CW01627807

The Complete Mrs Ravoon!

Pomes by Tim Rundall

Edited by:
Mike Hardaker
with an appreciation
of Tim Rundall by:
Jeremy Smith

wildaker

First Edition: 2022

Copyright © 2022, the Estate of Tim Rundall.

All rights reserved. No part of this publication may be reproduced, stored in or introduced into a retrieval system, or transmitted, in any form, or by any means without the prior written permission of the publisher.

This book is sold subject to the condition that it shall not, by way of trade or otherwise, be lent, resold, hired out, or otherwise circulated without the publisher's prior consent in any form of binding or cover other than that in which it is published and without a similar condition including this condition being imposed upon the subsequent purchaser.

Published in the United Kingdom by Wildaker.
Wildaker is an imprint of Palm Villa Studios (Pty) Ltd,
Cape Town, South Africa.

ISBN 978-2-87565-099-3

The Complete

Mrs Ravoon!

Tim Rundall (*aka* Slim Tim Slide) 1958–2022

A Life Lived in Music and Verse

Tim Rundall was a very talented guitarist, poet and music historian. Tim was born in London in 1958 and became a child model in the 1960s. He then moved to Oxfordshire and got involved in the music and underground scene, both there and in London. After a stint working for Brakspear's brewery and managing a hostel in Londonderry, Tim went to the University of Sussex in Brighton to study English, where he financed himself by busking and selling live tapes. He lived in Brighton till his death on 14 January 2022.

Music was a huge part of Tim's life whether playing solo; as a duo called Stinky and Stumpy with Trev Thoms (Inner City Unit), as guitarist and vocalist with the Brighton based trio, Thee Uncontrollables, or in later years, with Mick Farren and the reformed Deviants—including an appearance at Glastonbury Festival in 2011. In October 2015, Tim played a solo set at the Borderline supporting the Pink Fairies' last ever gig.

In the 1990's Tim published the Pink Fairies fanzine, Uncle Harry's City Kids (UHCK) and also curated three releases of Pink Fairies related material, *Silence of the Hams*, *Son of Ham* and *Hogwatch—For a Few Rashers More*. In 2004, Tim co-founded the Real Music Club in Brighton and played there regularly, including a number of benefit gigs. Tim also played on the 2010 Boss Goodman Testimonial Album: *Portobello Shuffle* supporting John Sinclair. More recently, Tim and Jaki Miles-Windmill produced 20 episodes of a radio show called *Sub-Reality Sandwich*, for Gonzo Multimedia.

As well as playing, Tim was a huge music fan and was immensely knowledgeable about the Pink Fairies and related acts, Bob Dylan, the cartoonist Edward Barker and many other eclectic musicians, writers and other creators.

Tim started writing the Mrs. Ravoon! saga in March 2016 and continued on an almost daily basis until April 2018. The poems (or *pomes* as they were known to Tim and his readers) were normally published daily together with associated images. He also wrote a series of pomes about a fictitious Indian snackbar run by Akbar. These had originally been written for his daughter Alice.

Tim Rundall died in Brighton, January 2022. He is sadly missed by friends and family. (JS)

Concerning Mrs Ravoon!

Mrs Ravoon! was not Tim's creation, but first saw the light of day in 1956, in a collection by Paul Dehr called *For Love and Money*. Since then, a number of writers have been drawn to her as a character (details are available on **www.mrsravoon.uk**) but none with the dedication—or, dare we say, the baroque imagination—of Tim Rundall. For the first half of the book, the pomes tend to have their own independent identity, but from pome 283—or thereabouts—they take on the nature of a cycle, which can be read almost as a verse novel. (MH)

(Editor's note: footnotes are the author's own, except where specified. They often refer to people who may or may not have been members of the Facebook group to which the pomes were posted at the time of a given pome's creation. This may confuse the reader. Or it may not.)

1.

’Twas soon after breakfast
Just before noon,
I purchased a paper
For half a doubloon,
There on page three
With her trusty bassoon,
Was a stark naked photo
...Of Mrs Ravoon!

2.

Through the sleepless night
That is over too soon,
Insomnia played
A monotonous tune
While out in the garden
A lust-crazed baboon,
Made furious love,
To Mrs Ravoon!

3.

Asleep in a bungalow,
Outside Dunoon,
Lay snoring, resplendent,
A handsome Dragoon,
While up in the sky,
From a hot-air balloon,
Waved the pink-bottomed figure
Of Mrs Ravoon!

4.

Clutched in the arms
Of a wandering Walloon,
Her face turned to purple
And then to maroon;
She strained, and then gasped
As if eating a prune,
The continent, self-contained
Mrs Ravoon!

5.

She slapped on her lipstick
And looked like a goon,
As she gazed into crystals
And wrote out a rune,
Obsessed by the future
Which passes so soon,
The pitiful figure—
Mrs Ravoon!

6.

In her birthday suit
She descended the dune,
Lit from behind
By the silvery moon,
While there on the beach
Sinatra did croon,
"It's now or never,
Mrs Ravoon!"

7.

Boiling her drugs
In a rusty old spoon,
Hawking, and spitting
Whilst humming a tune,
Writ by Lou Reed
Who had once made her swoon,
That decrepit degenerate
Mrs Ravoon!

8.

'Twas here yesterday
But has gone all too soon,
Read the sign that was held
By a silent buffoon,
So we threw him headfirst
Into the lagoon,
Where he lies on the bottom, with
Mrs Ravoon!

9.

The zookeeper yelled,
"It has been such a boon,
To discover that we had
Just one more Racoon,
I fear, had we not,
We'd've had to close soon.
Or been forced to exhibit
Mrs Ravoon!"

10.

Her scales fell away
From her skin. She had hewn
Great blocks from the ice,
In that freezing lagoon,
Nourished by only
A lone macaroon,
"I will survive," warbled
Mrs Ravoon!

11.

Sliding sideways she staggered,
Into the saloon,
Her handgun aimed
At an oil tycoon,
She knew that the end
Might be coming quite soon,
But she faced danger bravely,
Mrs Ravoon!

12.

Fearlessly leading,
Her wounded platoon,
Through wild mountain passes
And onward to Troon,
Hawking tobacco juice
At the spitoon,
That grizzled old veteran,
Mrs Ravoon!

13.

She sailed through the air,
As if in a cartoon,
Shot from a cannon,
She landed too soon,
Her body parts round
The airstrip were strewn,
Will you spare a plaster
For Mrs Ravoon?

14.

Emerging, unscathed,
From her dormant cocoon,
Moth-like, she fluttered,
With wings of maroon,
And danced in the sky,
'Neath a blood-red moon,
The ravenous, murderous,
Mrs Ravoon!

15.

Her favourite detective
Herbert McClune,
Was there on the telly,
Singing a tune,
It was one of her favourites:
Blue Moon
That nostalgic, neuralgic,
Mrs Ravoon!

16.
She scribbled her name
In the sand, 'neath the dune,
Her oxygen ebbing,
Wild-haired as a loon,
Was God but a merciless
Vacant poltroon?
Asked the existential
Mrs Ravoon!

17.
Crouching, half hidden
Atop a pontoon,
A siren sat singing
Au clair de la lune,
A passing young sailor,
In thrall of Neptune,
Jumped ship, to be ravished by
Mrs Ravoon!

18.
Hibernating through winter,
But waking in June,
Starving, she sucked on
The stone of a prune,
Which was red, though the flesh
Had long turned a dark broon,
Determined survivalist,
Mrs Ravoon!

19.

The headline in yesterdays
Herald Tribune,
Told us clearly that none
Were considered immune,
From the thief who sought
The unwashed pantaloon
Of the old undesirable,
Mrs Ravoon!

20.

A poet's small works
She was slow to impugn,
If the words were ill-chosen
And sometimes rough-hewn,
She was reading aloud
From a book of Sassoon,
The critical, erudite
Mrs Ravoon!

21.

Curled in a bush
Hiding from the monsoon,
Trembling with cold
As she watched the typhoon,
Disperse her possessions,
From here to Rangoon,
The anti-materialist
Mrs Ravoon!

The Sleep of Reason Produces Monsters: Francisco Goya

22.
Reaching the end
With a gasp and a swoon,
She struggled for breath
By the light of the moon,
Impaled on the spike
Of a whaling harpoon,
'Neath the dark silent water, lay
Mrs Ravoon!

23.
The joys of spring
And her signature tune,
Playing lightly upon
A contrabassoon,
Filled her ears at a moment
Quite inopportune,
For that hectically busy,
Mrs Ravoon!

24.
From old Oslo
To Brigadoon,
Wherever penguin eggs
Lay strewn,
Her name scratched
By her nails in stoon,
"I was here—
Mrs Ravoon!"

25.

From her lank greasy hair
She liked to festoon,
Strands of garbage and foodstuffs
Quite picayune,
Which remained there all year
From July through to June,
Stinking, with maggots, poor
Mrs Ravoon!

26.

After struggle and strife
She discovered the boon,
Of spending her life
In a hippy commune,
Timing her days
By the phase of the moon,
That unlikely pacifist
Mrs Ravoon!

27.

Alone on the island
Forced to consume,
Spiders and flies
Which she ate with a spoon,
She dreamt without hope
'Neath the shade of a poon,
There were no desert-discs, for
Mrs Ravoon!

28.

On the walls of her cave
She had scratched a cartoon,
Depicting her love
For a flea-bit baboon,
With whom she played endless
Games of pontoon
The sporting, yet bestial,
Mrs Ravoon!

29.

Bored of her hermitage—
Tired of the tune,
She emptied the
Overflowing spittoon,
Over the head
Of young Peter Noone,
There'll be *No milk today* for
Mrs Ravoon!

30.

As she finished dancing
The band ceased its tune,
The crowd went bananas
But fame came too soon,
And now, in retirement
Alone in Dunoon,
The snow settles gently on
Mrs Ravoon!

31.

She had pondered at length
Taking all afternoon,
As to whether 'twas wise
Or a trifle jejune
To bathe once a year
In the mighty monsoon
"It is so economical," mused
Mrs Ravoon!

32.

"If you push that button
It's nuclear doom,"
Cried her persistent assistant
From the back of the room
"You've less than four minutes,
You'd better leave soon,"
Cackled the nihilist
Mrs Ravoon!

33.

She scratched at her chin
With a sharpened doubloon,
She stole from a pirate
With her harpoon,
Whilst serving a jail sentence
Out in Rangoon,
The hirsute, yet particular
Mrs Ravoon!

34.
She disparaged equality
Born with silver-spoon,
Yet friend of Bethune,
Which perplexed her and vexed her
For he'd been a goon,
Unlucky in love, poor
Mrs Ravoon!

35.
Prospecting for gold
In the town of Cancun,
She found that the nuggets
Around her were strewn,
So she picked them all up;
It was so opportune,
No longer the penniless
Mrs Ravoon!

36.
The jitterbug contest
Was starting at noon,
The girls were all hoping
The singer would croon,
As the crowd gathered round
The band started a tune,
From outside, through a window, gazed
Mrs Ravoon!

37.

She passed all her days
In a haze and a swoon,
Lost in a reverie
Eating majoun,
Made with honey and hashish
Boiled in a spoon
Irresolute, dissolute
Mrs Ravoon!

38.

In the silence of night
Her ears would attune;
She could hear like a bat
As she skulked in the gloom,
Eating a stew
Which she made from cardoon,
The pathetic, ascetic,
Mrs Ravoon!

39.

The secret she kept
Had been seen by the moon,
That the children she'd borne
Had been sired by a loon,
She had captured when hiking
Across Camaroon,
The once lustful, now frigid
Mrs Ravoon!

40.

Glad that the party
Would be over soon,
She cackled with glee
As she burst a balloon,
Filled up with helium
By a Dragoon
Which made a soprano of
Mrs Ravoon!

41.

She went down to Haight Street
Just before Noon,
And scored her supplies
From an *Angel* called 'Coon,
Who rode by on his motorbike
Humming a tune:
She was *Born to be Wild*
Mrs Ravoon!

42.

In thrall of volcanoes
She skirted the dune,
As lava surrounded
Her feet, in a plume,
"It's better than pumice,"
The salesman crooned
To the charred, smoking, bones of
Mrs Ravoon!

43.

They hung her up high
From a tree outside Troon,
And left her there dangling
The whole afternoon,
But when gravity took her
And pulled her on doon,
The noose slowly tightened, on
Mrs Ravoon!

44.

Waving a six-gun
Just like Daniel Boone,
And staggering aimlessly
Round the saloon,
She shot ten more rounds
In the oil tycoon;
That murderous varmint
Mrs Ravoon!

45.

"You're a dolt and a dimwit
Not to mention poltroon,"
She wailed at the gypsy
Who'd read her fortune.
"I cannot eat spiders
Nor live in Dunoon."
But the fates were conspiring 'gainst
Mrs Ravoon!

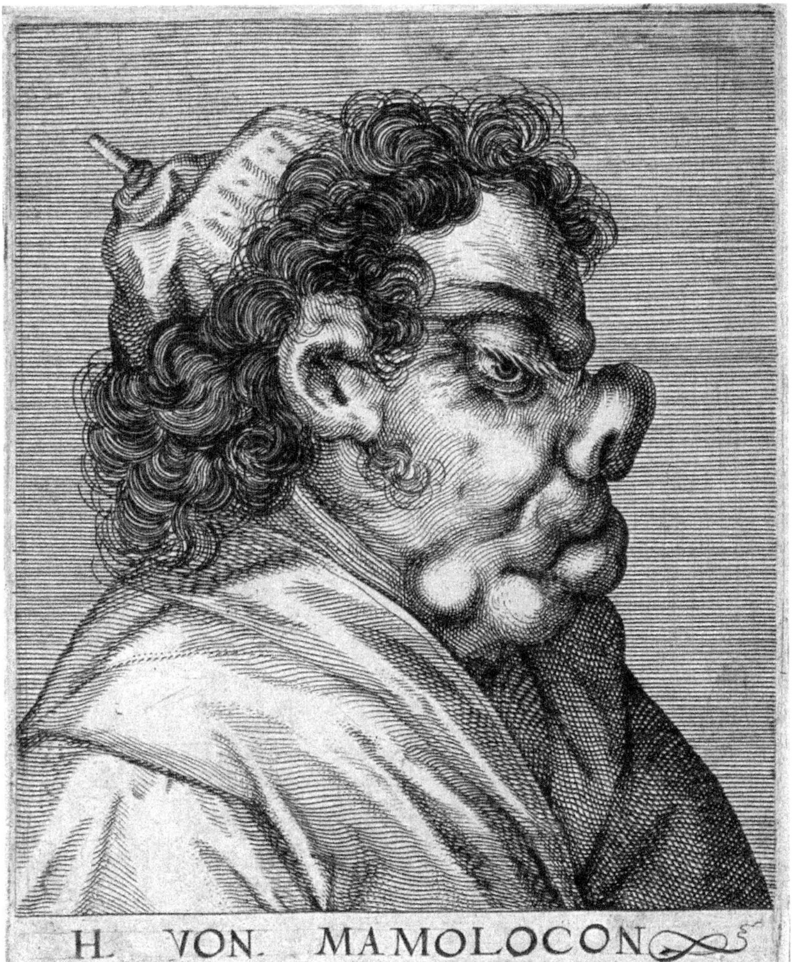

Herr von Mamolocon: attributed to D. Custos

46.
The bekilted sailor
Had caused her to swoon,
He'd seemed as remote
As the man in the moon,
Yet his demeanor, his musk
And his rod carved from poon,
Excited the adventurous
Mrs Ravoon!

47.
She married an ogre
Whose name was Verboon,
And hunted for meaning
By means of a rune,
And found it; alas,
Love departed too soon,
Leaving the shell of
Mrs Ravoon!

48.
These times, she reflected,
Have passed all too soon.
'Twas only on monday
I howled at the moon
Clad in the skin
Of a fresh-dead baboon,
Driven to madness,
Mrs Ravoon!

49.

In the vernacular
Her one eye was broon,
So she wore a monocle
And always looked doon,
She constantly whistled
But never in tune,
The spectacular, spectacled.
Mrs Ravoon!

50.

It is done, it is done
I have finished the tune,
I can rhyme no longer
In old Saskatoon,
My pen has run dry
Does the end come too soon?
I shall ponder no more
Upon Mrs Ravoon!

51.

She is back, in a mac
That's as black as a prune,
And she tears down the webs
Which around her are strewn;
With one eye she scans
A page of *Puckoon*,
Cackling, "I won't go quietly."
Mrs Ravoon!

52.
She abandoned her cave
And moved to Mattoon,
Where she hung from a tree
In a threadbare cocoon,
Surviving on bowls
Of spider lasoon
Which tickled the tastebuds, of
Mrs Ravoon!

53.
She injected herself daily
With bird Viromune,
But she'd taken so much
She was almost immune
As she squawked and she clattered
Her bones 'neath the moon,
She was barely a skeleton:
Mrs Ravoon!

54.
From the depths of the putrid
Stinking Lagoon,
Came a gurgling and fizzing
Like beer from DeKroon,
So she drank several gallons
And found, fairly soon,
She was dancing and singing
Mrs Ravoon!

55.
Completely bewildered
By transfer of Gruen,
She stumbled around
Till she fell down a dune,
She'd intended to meet up
With young Xiao Yun
But was hopelessly lost, poor
Mrs Ravoon!

56.
Though lacking in dress-sense
No one could impugn,
Her petticoats, edged
With the finest galloon,
There were stitches of gold
On her best pantaloon,
Yet her clothes were quite filthy, oh
Mrs Ravoon!

57.
She fashioned her gloves
From a long-dead racoon,
And used an old dogskin
To act as her shoon,
Scraps of old carcass
Around her were strewn,
The malodorous wardrobe of
Mrs Ravoon!

58.

She staved off starvation
With walnuts and huen,
Munching the shells
Till her teeth were a ruin,
As she walked back from India
Where once she had flewn,
Well-travelled, unravelled,
Mrs Ravoon!

59.

Her disdain knew no bounds
As she left the commune,
And sailed from the East
In her barrage balloon,
But one prick from a quill
In her hair, and *kaboom!*
Downward she spiralled,
Mrs Ravoon!

60.

The cold made her mean
And an icicle soon,
Made her vent her spleen
At the gods and the moon,
After all she had seen
Would death grip her so soon?
In the icy ravine, quivered
Mrs Ravoon![1]

---

1 By request of Steve Del Monte

61.

Dancing naked beneath
The Estonian moon,
She'd salted away
Nearly ten thousand kroon,
Which she spent giving succour
To Spotty Muldoon,
'Neath the flint beat the soft heart, of
Mrs Ravoon![2]

62.

An Iranian goatherd
Had once been her joon,
He'd bedecked her with jewellery
Which he had hewn,
From the walls of their cave
As he warbled this tune:
"I'll love you long time
Mrs Ravoon!"

63.

Screaming in Geordie
Supporting the Toon,
She'd bet her last tuppence
But they'd let her doon,
She was blind drunk on ten pints
Of Newcastle Broon,
The wise gave a wide berth to
Mrs Ravoon!

---

2 Thanks to Gary Wood

64.

Wrapped up in bandages
Fed with a spoon,
Nothing could disperse
The stifling gloom;
Suffering the curse
Of Tutankhamun,
Was that forgotten mummy
Mrs Ravoon!

65.

Working as a gumshoe
In the backstreets of Kowloon,
She'd seen the best and worst in life
And watched good fortune strewn,
Around like spat-out pits
From some long-discarded prune
The well-oiled, hard-boiled
Mrs Ravoon!

66a.

As radioactivity
Enveloped Dunoon,
Sanctioned by
General Bank I Moon,
A bag of green bones
Clacked and clicked out a tune:
'Twas the already glowing
Mrs Ravoon![3]

---

3 Thank you Andrew Stephen Thomas

66b.

As the afterglow shone
Eerie green 'pon the dune,
Dot Cotton's dog
Was exposing its poon,
The sodomite dalmatian of
General I Moon
Was torn twixt a poodle, and
Mrs Ravoon![4]

67.

The stagnant water
She was forced to consume,
Made her sick to the stomach
And turned her maroon,
So she headed south
And became a laffoon,
Which brought back the pallor to
Mrs Ravoon![5]

68.

The foolhardy folk
Living near Brigadoon,
Believed they could weather
The coming typhoon,
By rising above it
In a balloon;
On the ground, with a shotgun, stood
Mrs Ravoon!

---

4 With all due respect, and apologies, to Wilmot, the thespian dog

5 Laffoon: someone who dwells near a spring

69.
Specific instructions said
Not to exhume,
The putrefied body
That lay in the tomb,
Yet stood in the shadows
Clutching a spoon,
Was the starving, cadaverous
Mrs Ravoon!

70.
Desperate to travel
Far from Rangoon,
She hijacked a steam train;
An ill-maintained Thune,
The Norwegian instructions
Were all in cartoon,
Confusing that hobo,
Mrs Ravoon!

71.
The dapper young man
From the hippy commune,
Failed all the tests
On their brief honeymoon,
He was limp as a dishrag
She'd left him by June,
Her heart set on Spiderman—
Mrs Ravoon!

72.

In the post-apocalyptic
Ruins of Dunoon,
Crouching in the shadows
Glowing brighter than the moon,
A horrible mutation stirred
Beneath the rubble strewn;
Half-human, half-arachnid, it was
Mrs Ravoon!

73.

In the dark and swirling waters
Of the fast moving Karun,
The body of a goat-herd
Thought lost in the monsoon,
Drifted slowly out to sea; while,
Screeching like a loon,
By the river stood the murderess—
Mrs Ravoon!

74.

The necrotising scabs had turned
From green to dark maroon,
On twig-like legs which stuck out from
Below her pantaloon,
The spider bites she'd suffered
At the jail in Camaroon,
Spread poison through the blackened veins, of poor
Mrs Ravoon!

75.

To combat the stench
Coming from the lagoon,
Agreement was reached
To concoct a perfume,
An alliance was formed
'Twixt the people of Troon,
To milk the aroma of
Mrs Ravoon!

76.

In the baking contest
On that hot afternoon,
First prize was won
With a mauve macaroon;
The judge, passing judgement,
Collapsed in a swoon;
To his horror, the winner was
Mrs Ravoon!

76a

The secret recipe for
A mauve macaroon,
Involves crushing spiders
With the back of a spoon;
And mixing them up
With a hint of lasoon,
For a prize winning titbit, from
Mrs Ravoon!

77.

Crushing all the crystals
Rampaging o'er a rune,
Massacring whales
With a rusty old harpoon,
Marching at the head of
The devil's own platoon,
Like some plague from the Old Testament, stands
Mrs Ravoon!

78.

Her kif running low
She could make no majoun,
So chewed the pineal gland
From a baboon,
Which made her behave
Like a dribbling loon,
The insane, psychoactive,
Mrs Ravoon!

79.

Breaking her fast
In an old greasy spoon,
She yearned to be rescued
By some rich tycoon
Who would carry her off;
It was no picayune,
To the wholly unsatisfied
Mrs Ravoon!

80.

Tunelessly whistling
His signature tune,
Mrs R!'s latest conquest
Was nought but a loon,
She mimicked his tics
And was swift to lampoon,
His every fault, mean old
Mrs Ravoon!

81.

She'd courted the Sherriff
Down in Terhune,
That infamous township
In the county of Boone,
Where life was so cheap
And the dead were wide-strewn;
Their bones merely keepsakes, for
Mrs Ravoon!

82.

Playing billiards alone
In the silent saloon,
She whiled away
The whole afternoon,
Waiting in vain
For the wandering Maroon,
Who had run away swiftly, from
Mrs Ravoon!

83.

On a blasted heath
'Neath a blinding icy moon,
From a blighted tree
With a noose tied tight aroon,
With twitching bony limbs
And mottled clothes wide-strewn,
Hung a gasping throttled hag, crying "I'm
Mrs Ravoon!"

84.

Highly displeased when
A single doubloon,
Had bought her no pleasure
Nor moistened her prune,
It was unsatisfactory
But things would change soon,
'Neath the stern ministrations of…
Mrs Ravoon!

85.

The fact that the officer
Was a buffoon,
Turned out to be
An absolute boon,
There was no doubt of guilt
So 'twas most opportune
That he perjured himself, trying
Mrs Ravoon!

86.

Hiding beneath
The broken pontoon,
In the still of the night
She was swift to attune,
Her ears to the rush
Of the pirate's harpoon,
Diving for cover—
Mrs Ravoon!

87.

A burning sensation combined with some gas
Were the signs of her imminent brune,
She rushed for the outhouse, and wearing a mask
With a skid, she then rolled down the dune,
Until finally seated, she gasped with relief
And whistled *Au clair de la lune,*
Though the stench was horrendous and beyond belief, 'twas exquisite to
Mrs Ravoon!

88.

The crabs bit her feet
In the bay of Cancun,
And scuttled, disgusted,
Away in the gloom,
Old seaweed and starfish
Were used to festoon
The cadaverous features, of
Mrs Ravoon!

89.

The tanks of disease, which she kept in her cave,
Were the talk of the whole of Dunoon,
"Bacterial warfare is mine," she would rave,
"And none of you folk are immune."
She ate ebola for breakfast, before it ate her;
Stirred with a germ-ridden spoon,
Buboes and leprosy were but small beer, for filthy old
Mrs Ravoon!

90.

Reeking of gin
Distilled in Mattoon,
Diluted with water
From the lagoon,
She reeled back yelling,
"This glass is too schoon."
For she revelled in filthiness:
Mrs Ravoon!

91.

Justin Bieber fell off stage
Last night in Saskatoon
And as the crowd raised up their iPhones
No-one knew the tune
Least of all the singer
Who may as well have been baboon
As a replacement with more talent, I'd vote
Mrs Ravoon!

92.

"I must have some spiders, I must have some gin,
I simply can't wait until June,
I'm hungry, I'm thirsty, my head's in a spin,
I'm obsessed by the silver galloon
That runs down the trouser leg, into the shoes
Of that dark and mysterious dragoon,
I shall have him, I must, I'll seduce him with booze," mused the
frustrated
Mrs Ravoon!

93.

The quiet of the evening was split by a scream
That came from a rampant racoon,
Who was sick to the stomach of love's young dream
It longed for more action, and soon,
In frustration it raged and declared, "This is not,
Quite what I would consider a boon."
As its poor little body was hurled in a pot, it was dinner for
Mrs Ravoon!

94.

Give this spot to blind Pugh
And moan softly the tune,
That carried us onwards
That bleak afternoon,
As sea wind tore our skin
And dead mermaids did croon,
Their skeletons gathered, by
Mrs Ravoon!

95.
Pounding the graveyard
On the outskirts of Troon,
In one hand a spade,
In the other a spoon,
Dancing deliriously
Under the moon,
Devil drums shake the bones, of
Mrs Ravoon!

96.
At the end of the match the ref waved his arm
And the crowd sang a victory tune,
Trouble came quickly, as keen to cause harm,
There stood a murderous hoon,
Whose complexion was sickly, whose breath smelt of booze
Whose judgement was swift to impugn,
She skulked in the shadows, screaming abuse, that hooligan
Mrs Ravoon!

97.
A beautiful mouse
Said "Hello," to the moon,
Squeaking sweet-nothings
In the ear of its joon,
A rat left some cheese
On the floor by the troon,
Awaiting the picnic of
Mrs Ravoon!

98.
On the beach were bleached bones
Picked clean by Neptune;
High above glowed the planet
Outshining the moon;
It's retrograde action
Foretold ill-fortune,
For the pirates who'd plotted 'gainst
Mrs Ravoon!

99.
The lumps in her armpits
Were turning maroon,
As she dripped with buboes
On the trip from Kowloon;
Infected by rats
Her auto-immune
Infected them back! The reciprocal
Mrs Ravoon!

100.
The fistfuls of laxatives
Prescribed by Dr Kuhn,
Were swift to alleviate
And acted as a prune,
Her bowels were now so loose
That she resembled a spittoon,
The quite convulsive, most repulsive
Mrs Ravoon!

101.
Voting *Leave* she had reason
To regret it fairly soon,
As the locals gathered sticks and stones
And placards saying "Doon—
We can't abide the stink, nor hue,
Of your boyfriend from Cancun."
Would Brexit mark the exit, of
Mrs Ravoon?

102.
Sailing merrily through the air
In her hot-air balloon,
Dropping bags of spider-eggs
On the people of Dunoon,
Shouted out most vehemently,
"The webs will catch you soon."
There was no bunting, for the people-hunting
Mrs Ravoon!

103.
Ancient wisdom was hidden
In old Camaroon,
Carried by hoot-owls
Encoded in tune;
Played in the night
On a contrabassoon,
Bringing power and delight to
Mrs Ravoon!

104.

From a distant galaxy
They came to the lagoon,
Having heard the plaintive sound of people
Barking at the moon.
Disembarking from their spacecraft,
Stepping onto the pontoon,
The aliens met their nemesis in
Mrs Ravoon!

105.

One hundred years on
From the days of Sassoon,
Bitter traces of smoke
Still hung in late June
Surely 'twas time now
To change mankind's tune?
Mused the unlikely pacifist
Mrs Ravoon!

106.

She stood on the bridge clutching her head
As volcanic smoke rose in a plume,
Pondering life as she counted the dead
And wondering if there was room,
For another small body beneath all the lava
Among all the bones that were strewn
Around her as if they were in Balaclava; the traumatised
Mrs Ravoon!

107.

As the aliens left they cast a strange light
On the waters that flow past Dunoon,
Illuminating creatures that would rather take flight
Than be washed up to die 'neath a dune,
Hurtling back to the planet they came from
Bearing bad news written doon
On scraps of paper they'd found on the shore
Scribbled by
Mrs Ravoon!

108.

She dined on the finest
Roasted baboon,
Gin-marinated
And served with cardoon,
A side dish of spiders
And breakfast at noon,
Made the whole day a banquet, for
Mrs Ravoon!

109.

The bell on the mountain
Rang out of tune,
The clapper was cracked
And had been since June,
Smashed in the violence
Of a summer typhoon,
Reflecting the temper of
Mrs Ravoon!

Unknown photographer, c.1910

110.

Surrounded by opossum
Which she mistook for racoon,
She fed them all with spider stew
From a sliver spoon,
Until they were fat enough,
(Which would be fairly soon),
To make a stew all by themselves, for
Mrs Ravoon!

111.

Loyal to no-one, armed with an axe,
Bearing a truncheon, and soon,
Mumbling in voodoo of unproven facts
She'll fight with the craziest loon.
After her luncheon, her face just like wax,
Several gallons of gin make her croon
O'er her enemies' carcasses lain on their backs, drunk and violent—
Mrs Ravoon!

112.

The escapees faced starvation
As they fled the barracoon,
And while stranded in the jungle
Surrounded by gaboon,
They survived by eating spiders
And the flesh of raw racoon,
But the stench of their meal saw them recaptured—their fate?
Mrs Ravoon!

113.

A black and mighty stallion
Slid sideways down the dune,
The saddle made from spider fur
As was the bridoon,
The cloaked and fearsome rider
Seemed a gaunt and headless goon,
'Neath the skeletal guise, shone the evil eyes of
Mrs Ravoon!

114.

The rescue party searched all night
Led by a skilled Walloon,
But come the dawn there'd been no sight
Of the tourist from Rangoon,
Whose skeletal remains made a clicking noise—
Whose demise had come so soon,
Clasped to the wheezing bony breast of
Mrs Ravoon!

115.

An avalanche came down the slope
Of rocks which had been hewn,
By villagers who'd dug a cave
To escape from the monsoon,
But it was taken over
And turned into a commune,
Of insects, bats, and feral cats; and
Mrs Ravoon!

116.
While collecting local insects
In the small town of Burgoon,
Her amorous eye soon fell upon
A handsome octaroon,
Whose obsession with arachnids
Did not help him rise aboon,
The web of lust and intrigue spun by…
Mrs Ravoon!

117.
A diet of spiders
Grew wearisome soon,
But constructing a web
By the light of the moon,
Caught plenty of flies;
Maggots, eggs, and cocoon
Which varied the diet of
Mrs Ravoon!

118.
Worshipping dead gods
From a temple in Kowloon,
Believers sacrificed their young
To the spirits from aboon,
They expected retribution from
The dark side of the moon,
But vengeance came from the vaguely human
Mrs Ravoon!

118a.

The eggs of a vulture
Combined with cardoon,
Bubbled away in
Oil of cohune
You could smell it for miles
It was rank as racoon
But it sated the hunger of
Mrs Ravoon!

119.

The voice of God rang out
Over the whole town of Dunoon,
It rained and boomed and caused concern
The entire afternoon,
It burned some kilts, someone on stilts,
At night blocked out the moon,
Everyone knew who was to blame—
Mrs Ravoon!

120.

From the tubes in the lab
Where she worked with the Woon,
Noxious fumes had brought nausea
To the folks of Rangoon;
Choking and sweating
In the gaseous plume,
They cursed the experiments of
Mrs Ravoon!

121.

The accursed accordion
Would not stay in tune,
But the mad mystic hammering
Of the Djun Djun,
Was cause for crazed dancing
'Neath a cold mocking moon;
In a frenzy of voodoo, drummed
Mrs Ravoon!

122.

Sharp bursts of static
Disturbed the lagoon,
The ancient wireless
Lay broken and strewn,
Rusty components
Hung from the dioon,
There was radio-silence for
Mrs Ravoon!

123.

In her youth she was fond of whisky and fags
Which she shared with the would-be dragoon,
They coughed and spluttered, as they puttered
Around on the dank lagoon,
But she was more hardy, he was too tardy
He'd played her for a goon
And now a hangover is all that's left over, from the young love of
Mrs Ravoon!

124.

Whirling like a dervish
In the chilly afternoon,
She had the flexibility
Of an epizoon,
There was no finer dancer
Not even the Shiogoon,
Who oversaw the dance troupe starring
Mrs Ravoon!

125.

The collection of bugs in the back of the cave
Had been gathered from all over Troon,
With bitter reluctance she finally gave
A few to her pet gaboon,
When it gobbled too many she'd rant and she'd rave
Saying, "Why can't you stick with matzoon?"
Apart from these morsels nothing could stave, off the hunger of
Mrs Ravoon!

126.

The goatherd was descended
From Abdul Khan Badoon,
His aspect was so handsome
He resembled a triune,
His body almost godlike,
His mind that of a loon;
The perfect combination for
Mrs Ravoon!

127.

Diving for crustaceans
In the river at Fordoun,
The icy waters caused her skin
To wrinkle like a prune,
But the special cream she kept
Beside the bait in her seroon,
Re-moisturised the leathery hide of
Mrs Ravoon!

128.

Using a machete to cut
The cane so widely strewn,
Spattered by the sugary sap
That oozed from the ratoon,
Insects licked her sticky skin
As the stains turned slowly broon,
On the fly- and oil-based suntan, of
Mrs Ravoon!

129.

When asked if she had *Seen the light,*
She pointed at the moon,
As a small but deadly spider
Scuttled round the room,
She was clinging to a satellite
Around the apolune,
High above the lunar surface—
Mrs Ravoon!

130.

Raised by a nanny
On rancid bagoong,
Unable to spell
Or to render a tune,
Except for a painful
Au clair de la lune,
Such was the childhood of
Mrs Ravoon!

131.

In the depths of the cave
Was a hidden ceroon,
Which contained the dried flesh
Of a long-dead baboon,
The day of its opening
Would be coming quite soon,
If the stars were in alignment for
Mrs Ravoon!

132.

She'd eaten too many insects
So had taken a dose of puccoon:
The bugs then all violently left her
And some of them flew round the room,
But they found that there was no escaping
For she'd caused many webs to festoon,
Her cave so she caught them and later,
They were re-eaten by
Mrs Ravoon!

133.

Never one to be
A part of an anderoon,
Always on the lookout
For any stray tycoon,
That she could take advantage of
Or somehow importune,
Nobody could manipulate like
Mrs Ravoon!

134.

Seeking refuge in the desert
From the worst of the monsoon,
Then heading slowly coastwards
Where she stole a frigatoon,
She set sail for dear old Scotland
And her home by the lagoon,
Where whisky drowned the loneliness of
Mrs Ravoon

135.

In the islands she found friendship
With a disreputable sheboon,
Who with admirable fortitude
Came there from Cameroon,
Across the endless ocean
Clutching only one doubloon,
Which was subsequently stolen, by
Mrs Ravoon!

136.
She hid inside a filthy pit
Beneath a plenilune,
Sheltered from the probing eyes
Of any passing goon,
Breathing through a tube that ran
From an entrance, sublacune,
Into the chilly cave, the domicile of
Mrs Ravoon!

137.
Falling sick from eating
Some fish from the lagoon
Growing pale, alarming pink
And then turning maroon,
Infected by the germs
Of some infernal hydrozoon,
Regurgitation was the sorry lot of
Mrs Ravoon!

138.
As the rain poured down
The streets of Dunoon,
Were all washed clean
Of detritus and soon,
It was time to erect
The blocking tappoon
That protected the lair, of
Mrs Ravoon!

138 redux.

As the rain poured down
On the streets of Dunoon,
They were all washed clean
Of detritus but soon,
It seemed that nobody
Had a tappoon
They'd been stolen, the suspect?
Mrs Ravoon!

139.

Standing on the scaffold
Overlooking Troon,
Pondering a life ill-spent
And wondering if soon,
She could bribe the hangman
With her purse of ducatoon
Seconds felt like lifetimes, for
Mrs Ravoon!

140.

They'd buried the body
'Neath a salt-sodden dune,
Hoping in vain that it
Would not be found soon,
But the action of lightning
Fate and assorted protozoon,
Begat the resurrection of
Mrs Ravoon!

141.

It was a sad day when hunger
Made her eat her pet racoon,
But she perked up with a hair-do—
Free—from Vidal Sassoon,
It took five hours to untangle
Her locks, but what a boon
To the penny-pinching confidence of
Mrs Ravoon!

142.

Sailing through the clouds
In a big hot-air balloon,
Seeking with binoculars
Outcrops of jargoon,
With which to fashion fetishes
To fondle like a loon,
Was the gaunt-faced voodoo priestess, known as
Mrs Ravoon!

143.

The goatherd had died slowly
Beneath the harvest moon,
He'd ignored the many warnings
From the likes of Laocoon,
His life-sap had been drained
Like so much honey from a spoon,
And his body then discarded, by
Mrs Ravoon!

144.

An emotionless fugue
Held her on the pontoon,
As her eyes fixed upon
The drowning dragoon,
Who'd already swallowed
Much of the lagoon;
"It was fun while it lasted," mused
Mrs Ravoon!

145.

Living cheaply was important
She was sly as a gaboon,
Resenting every cent in rent
Paid out to the patroon,
Which takes us to her present lair
On the outskirts of Dunoon,
Where, free to rave inside her cave, squats
Mrs Ravoon!

146.

A cold and cruel winter
Decimated the commune,
Just nine-tenths were left alive to
Tithe the fundiloon,
But the one to save the day
With her treasured last testoon,
Was that most unlikely aphrodite
Mrs Ravoon!

147.

In an effort to reduce the size
Of his disgusting epiploon,
A plan of action was devised
By the mayor of Kowloon,
Each morning he would rise at six
To perform a rigadoon,
For his apoplectic dance instructor
Mrs Ravoon

148.

In a home-made pair of dancing shoes
Made from skinned baboon,
Whose meat had all been long consumed
In meals of lahmacun,
Measured steps were taken
On the walls encircling Troon,
In a danse-macabre of ill-intent, by
Mrs Ravoon!

149.

Flying higher than could be achieved
Using a rockoon,
Escaping from the atmosphere
And heading for the moon,
She realised that no sound came
As she played her tenoroon,
In the icy maw of empty space hung
Mrs Ravoon!

150.
Striking fear into the hearts
Of the people in Rangoon,
Creeping through the orient
Possessed by a kitsune,
Seemingly the harbinger
Of deadly ill-fortune
Everyone was justly terrified, of
Mrs Ravoon!

151.
She had at her disposal
A flock of nyctibune,
To suck the milk from pregnant goats
Which she would then consume,
That the kids would then all perish,
Was a neat and timely boon;
It meant there was fresh meat to eat, for
Mrs Ravoon!

152.
Inclement weather was threatening the lives
Of everyone that afternoon,
Thousands would perish but one would survive
The outrageously powerful typhoon,
Pushing aside all the others
Leaping headfirst into the Karun
With no thought for the children nor for their mothers, the cold-hearted
Mrs Ravoon!

153.
Liking them young
And in need of a prune,
Seeking out those
Who she could make swoon,
She'd set her eyes
On a hirsute gazoon,
Who'd succumb to the scissors of
Mrs Ravoon!

154.
The gramophone played
A peculiar tune,
A god-awful version
Of her favourite, *Blue Moon,*
So she smashed it to pieces
As it played a chiptune,
"Bring back mono," cried
Mrs Ravoon!

155.
Despising the goat-herd
She abandoned the room,
Pondering how to despatch him
And soon,
Sliced off by a freshly sharpened
Spadroon,
His head was collected by
Mrs Ravoon!

156.

Though beauty was scarce
Usually lit by the moon,
Outside the cave
Was a tended floroon,
Sprouted from seeds
That were brought from Cancun,
By the strangely green-fingered
Mrs Ravoon!

157.

Her eyes caught the mirror
As she passed in the gloom,
Her bone-structure fragile,
Her hair filthy broon,
Yet a small glint of light
Flashing from a godroon,
Brought out the best in
Mrs Ravoon!

158.

Hacking up phlegm
Into her spitoon,
Sucking her pipe
Which she would petune,
Germs stood no chance
Nor did perfume
In the encrusted lungs, of
Mrs Ravoon!

159.

The scratching of the sackcloth
Made her gibber like a goon,
Flakes of skin kept sloughing off
And lay around her strewn,
Like pink and scabrous petals
How she longed for some shalloon,
To ease the itch that tormented poor
Mrs Ravoon!

160.

With a moué of distaste
At the smell from the bagoong,
She turned and left the market
And walked out of Kowloon,
It only took ten seconds
For her to reattune,
No one could fault the bat-like ears, of
Mrs Ravoon!

160a.

Enjoying synaeasthesia
She tasted the maroon,
And marvelled at the multi-levelled
Music of the moon,
The sweet smell of many textures
Emanated from a spoon,
As she watched time marching backwards; lucky
Mrs Ravoon!

161.
Blasted by the desert sands
Blown by the simoon,
With aching feet and shaking hands
She rested 'neath a dune,
Spying an oasis
Reflecting a half moon,
Crawling desperately to quench her thirst, was
Mrs Ravoon!

162.
Recoiling instinctively
From the dragoon,
As he signalled his comrades
With his spontoon,
Reaching out
For her favoured harpoon,
The stench of his blood tickled
Mrs Ravoon!

163.
A large cask of brandy
Washed up 'neath the dune,
That lay by the side
Of the putrid lagoon,
Yet nothing could force out
The ancient tampoon,
And so it stays, hidden, by
Mrs Ravoon!

164.

Determined to fly
Her brand new kytoon,
And keeping an eye
On the coming typhoon,
Her test pilot would be
The fearless huboon
Who was blindly devoted to
Mrs Ravoon!

165.

Looting wrecks on the rocks
Where the cargo lay strewn,
And plundering bodies
Ill-lit by the moon,
Under threat from a cutlass
The young picaroon
Knew too well the intentions of
Mrs Ravoon!

166.

Yearning by day
For a small puftaloon,
Dreaming by night
Of just one macaroon,
There was no nutrition
But a single teaspoon
Of arachnid juice, for
Mrs Ravoon!

167.

Living anonymously
In a penthouse in Cancun,
Was a highly suspicious
And unpleasant terceroon
Who was known to speculate
Whilst high on cacoon
That he might be the offspring, of
Mrs Ravoon![6]

---

6 Responses to 167:

An oh how they danced
The little children of Stone 'enge
Beneath a haunted moon
For fear that daybreak
Might bring
Baby Ravoon! —Andrew Stephen Thomas

Midnight cry, child born.
Illicit child, treated with scorn.
Progeny of Ravoon! —Alun Webb

Midnight cry, child born
Illicit, treated with scorn.
Dark spawn of Ravoon! —Sylvia Bestwick, turning Alun's pome into a proper Haiku: 5-7-5

168.

The children had all long been sold
To a trader in Kowloon,
Their whereabouts a mystery
Their future gone too soon,
But after years of fruitless search
Vengeful eyes unshewn,
Fixed upon the unrepentant
Mrs Ravoon!

169.

She'd sold them for a pittance
And set sail that afternoon,
Having spent the lot on opium
And a trip to Camaroon,
But her need was all consuming
And the drugs ran out too soon,
Leaving the quaking barren wreck, of
Mrs Ravoon!

170.

A small family gathering
In a cave outside Dunoon,
Seemed to go quite swimmingly
As bagpipes played a tune,
The dancing went on all night long—
A waltz, a rigadoon—
While outside in the icy rain, fumed
Mrs Ravoon!

171.
Beside herself with fury
Her few possessions strewn,
Outside the entrance to the cave
And under rocks ill-hewn,
Invasion of her privacy
Threatened to distune,
The scant mental stability of
Mrs Ravoon!

172.
Breakfast would be plentiful;
A stew of spiced raccoon,
Bubbled in a cauldron
And was tempered with cardoon,
Ghost chillies had been added too,
Enough to melt a spoon;
In the corner munching spiders, glowered
Mrs Ravoon!

173.
One of the boys had grabbed a fork
Along with a sharpened spoon,
He drank deep, replaced the cork
And reached for his harpoon,
The populace could only gawk
And hope that fairly soon,
The grudge match would be settled, by the son of
Mrs Ravoon!

173a.

Deepinder must have been in a dream,
Or living in some kind of swoon,
From whenever it was that we started this group
Up to now, and right through June,
It seems he has no knowledge of
The evil cackling croon,
That emits from the lips, and shoots from the hips, of our
sponsor—
Mrs Ravoon!

173b.

R__ L_______ must be so glad
He must think it a boon,
To find he's in good company
And not be all aloon,
But in the future we all trust
He'll not be such a goon,
As to ignore the daily news, on
Mrs Ravoon!

173c.

Amanda Davies seems so blue
And lacking in a tune,
Let's hope she's not averse to verse
'Cos this one's none too soon,
I'm hopeful she will be quite pleased
And blow up a balloon,
To celebrate her inclusion in the tale of
Mrs Ravoon!

173d.

There's something nice about Sarah Price,
That turns me into a loon,
Is it her hair, all up there
Or my repressed desire to spoon?
Whatever it is I want lots more
But the moment's ne'er too soon
To warn against a close encounter, with the author of
Mrs Ravoon!

173e.

He sure knows how to yack on, Hakon,
But despite that he's a boon,
He shaves himself especially
For parties that are threwn,
And grins and laughs, takes photographs,
And though he's sometimes doon,
His happy demeanour contrasts with the meaner, scowl of
Mrs Ravoon![7]

---

7 *Editor's note: pomes 173a–e refer to members, present and former, of the small Facebook group in which the Mrs Ravoon! pome cycle was first published.*

174.
Filled with ire and rancour
And itching like a loon,
To send her offspring far away,
To Brisbane or Rangoon,
"What did I do to deserve this?"
She wailed at the moon,
The blasted heath heard the gnashing teeth, of
Mrs Ravoon!

175.
A dark mysterious stranger
Stands upon the dune,
That lies beside the wasteland
On the outskirts of Dunoon,
Does he bear ill tidings?
Did he rise from the lagoon?
Trepidation tests the steely nerve, of
Mrs Ravoon!

176.
The stranger came up to the cave
Screeching like a loon,
Frightening the children
Who receded in the gloom,
While watching from a distance
Dressed in her pantaloon,
Aglow with admiration, was
Mrs Ravoon!

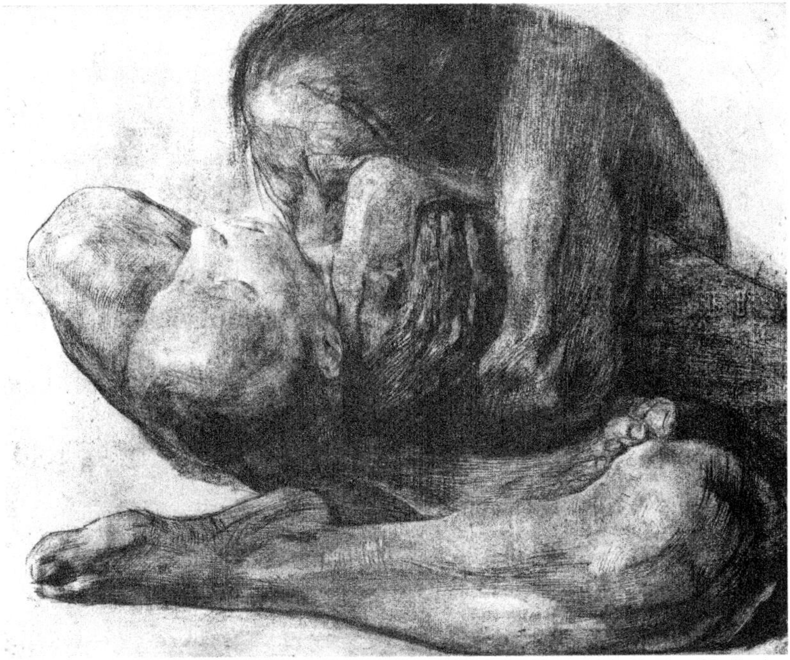

Frau mit totem Kind: Käthe Kollwitz

177.
Grabbing her in his hairy arms
Like some large virile baboon,
He hurled her body to the floor;
It was clear that pretty soon,
Lustful moaning would be heard
All across Dunoon,
As he skilfully thawed the cold resolve, of
Mrs Ravoon!

178.
In the grip of strong emotion
As alien as some moon,
That orbited round Jupiter
At one with the vacuum,
Of icy space, unrecognised
And yet, there in Dunoon,
Lustful tremors shook the bones of
Mrs Ravoon!

179.
Flushed in her post-coital glow
First pink, and then maroon,
Little drops of acidic sweat
Let out a strange perfume,
Which unnerved the handsome stranger
As he staggered round the room,
Would he survive or become a meal for
Mrs Ravoon!?

180.

The children were all huddled in fear
Shivering under the moon,
As they strained to lend an ear
To the strangers strangled croon,
Their hopes of survival seemed so slim
Yet they yearned to escape, and soon,
But the way was barred by the snoring bodies, of the stranger and
Mrs Ravoon!

181.

A steaming cauldron filled the cave
With a strange acrid perfume,
Little bones were bubbling up;
She would be eating soon,
But what was in that ghastly stew
Which smelt worse than bagoong?
The stranger or the progeny of
Mrs Ravoon!?

182.

The homeless stranger'd wandered in,
With neither plate nor spoon,
Dependant on the kindness
Of those who lived by the lagoon,
But the fish had all mutated
And washed up dead amongst the spume,
While a greenish glow illuminated
Mrs Ravoon!

183.

She'd always found it hard to share
So from the arctic to Rangoon,
Domestic life was something that
She had forcibly eschewn,
But this rugged stranger, firm yet fair,
Lit up the strangest tune,
In that black heart deep in the lair, of
Mrs Ravoon!

184.

A stream of rampant pheromones
Wafted across the room,
Emitting from the stranger
With a sweet musky perfume
But was it all too good to last?
With the waning of the moon
Creeping doubt gave pause for thought, to
Mrs Ravoon!

185.

A belch of satisfaction
Broke the silence of the room,
The cooking fire had long gone out;
The chill was like a tomb,
Tiny bones lay scattered round
With half-eaten cardoon,
There was no sign of the children, of
Mrs Ravoon!

186.

The handsome stranger picked his teeth
With a bone like a harpoon,
Dislodging masticated flesh
And grinning like a loon,
Tired of eating spiders
He had slowly changed his tune,
His moral compass now destroyed, by
Mrs Ravoon!

187.

Weeks passed by in silence
Like phases of the moon,
It was soon September
When it had only just been June,
Mornings brought on nausea
There were twitchings in her womb,
Would something unforeseen emerge, from
Mrs Ravoon!?

188.

Suffering daily
She took to the saloon,
Knocking back endless shots of hootch
Which she paid for in Kroon,
Her mind was quite bewildered
Her state inopportune,
Would spent passion be the nemesis of
Mrs Ravoon!?

189.

She cursed the handsome stranger
Who had brought her close to ruin,
The last traces of attraction
Stumbled from the room,
There was nobody more desperate
In the region of Dunoon,
Than the once selected, now infected
Mrs Ravoon!

190.

'Twas an ill-wind of nausea
That hit like a typhoon,
And signalled the conclusion
Of the briefest honeymoon,
How she wished she could lay eggs
Or simply spin a nice cocoon,
As nature took its sweet revenge, on
Mrs Ravoon!

191.

Strange new appetites emerged
And forced her to consume,
Insects of outlandish type,
Raw fish and boiled racoon,
A simple meal of spiders legs
Was a memory jejune,
That evoked a bleak nostalgia in poor
Mrs Ravoon!

192.

Groaning on the stony floor
And writhing in the gloom,
Clutching at her abdomen
While cursing her fortune,
How she wished now that the stranger
Had never reached Dunoon,
But perished somewhere far away from
Mrs Ravoon!

193.

She drank a whole pot of raspberry-leaf tea
Hoping it might bring the boon,
Of ending her torment and bringing relief
Which surely must come pretty soon,
But nothing could stop the impending event
As she tore out her hair like a loon,
From all sides disaster seemed to close in, on the now balding
Mrs Ravoon!

194.

The doctor she called
Proved to be a buffoon,
Offering aspirin
He was immune,
To her pleas for opium
Fresh from Kowloon,
The one thing that might comfort
Mrs Ravoon!

195.
The midwife arrived and said
"Just lie doon.
We shall harvest these eggs
By the light of the moon,
There'll be no nonsense
Don't bother to swoon."
Which astounded the ill-prepared
Mrs Ravoon!

196.
The pushing and groaning continued
All night till the next afternoon,
When there suddenly came an outpouring
That turned the midwife maroon,
Hundreds of spiderlings scampered
Free of that desolate womb,
Yet also a cry no-one could deny from a small clone of
Mrs Ravoon!

197.
Its sex was indeterminate
It radiated gloom,
The face was reminiscent
Of a half-obscured blue moon,
Little teeth protruded
As it gurgled like a goon,
Nobody congratulated
Mrs Ravoon!

198.

Wiry hair grew from its skull
Down past its epiploon,
Its bulging eyes and flapping ears
Resembled boiled lardoon,
No beauty was apparent
In the face of this quadroon,
There'd be no bonny-baby prize for
Mrs Ravoon!

199.

Like some underwater creature
Found in the lagoon,
Tentacled and wafting
An ammonia perfume,
Barnacle encrusted
And washed up on the dune,
'Twas hard to love the new-born child, of
Mrs Ravoon!

200.

A head that looked like Churchill
Each toe a little spoon,
Endless all-night screeching
Worse than a baboon,
Scabs that left great craters
like those upon the moon,
Weeping sores, hungry jaws... oh poor
Mrs Ravoon!

201.

Awake from dusk to daybreak
Dozing until noon,
Daydreaming of long-lost days
Back in Cameroon,
Jerked back to the present
By the stench from the lagoon,
A restless hungry feeling gnawed at
Mrs Ravoon!

202.

Spiderlings were scuttling
All about the room,
Their little webs a-twinkling
As if edged with gold galloon,
In the sharp light of the morning
As they formed an odd platoon,
To defend their new-born sibling from
Mrs Ravoon!

203.

Half crazed from lack of sleep
Raving like a loon,
Smashing down old cobwebs
With a long and dusty broom,
Squashing spiders underfoot
Until her soles turned broon,
Infanticide obsessed the mind of
Mrs Ravoon!

204.
Scampering out of the cave
And onto the pontoon,
There were spiders everywhere
Some fell in the lagoon,
And were swiftly gobbled up by fish
Like nuts in a saloon,
While silhouetted 'gainst the sun stood
Mrs Ravoon!

205.
Fists raised in defiance
With an improvised batoon,
Half hidden in the shadows
Of a bright but waning moon,
Staggering round blindly
And humming out of tune,
Hell bent with ill intent, was
Mrs Ravoon!

206.
Plucked out of its fetid crib
By trembling hands immune,
To sentiment or motherhood—
The hands of a huboon,
A tiny cry emitted
From that babe of ill-fortune,
No good would ever come to it, from
Mrs Ravoon!

207.

Heating up the cauldron
To a long and tuneless croon,
Stirring up the liquor
With her ancient rusty spoon,
Oil bubbled furiously
Mixed with old matzoon,
Maniacal fervour overtook
Mrs Ravoon!

207a.[8]

A baking show was taking place
That very afternoon,
Mary Berry would be there—
Her first time in Dunoon!
Malevolently cackling
O'er a poisoned macaroon
Was the nemesis of Mary B,
Mrs Ravoon!

207b.

At the height of the contest Mrs R!
Along with her friend Brenda,
Grabbed the judges by their necks
And chucked them in a blender,
Reducing them to sodden gore
They then went on a bender,
And posted off the judges' bones
Marked *Return to sender*

---

8 In response to comments, I made up the following two; Brenda is a mate of Sylvia

208.

She jellified the babe by boiling
Under a gibbous moon,
And sold the chopped-up morsels
To the sweet shop in Dunoon,
They proved to be most popular,
Were all sold that afternoon;
In the cave counting her new-found wealth, sat
Mrs Ravoon![9]

209.

The jitterbug contest was held once again
In the Nissen hut by the lagoon,
There was laughter and revelling, buffet and band
The fun went on all afternoon,
The prospect of dancing was hard to resist;
Itchy feet made her twitch in the gloom,
But nobody there was willing to share their dance card with
Mrs Ravoon![10]

209a.

A skeleton horse cantered along
The busy main street of Dunoon,
Ridden by a flame haired temptress
Whose outfit was mud-spattered broon,
Over the sound of its hooves came a melody
Played on an ancient bassoon
Raising the question of who had played it; Sarah, or
Mrs Ravoon!

---

9 Inspired—if that is the word—by Sylvia's reference to Jelly Babies

10 In response to a comment by Sarah

210.

Zipping round the dancefloor
Like a coffee-crazed baboon,
Dancing to the jungle drums
That echoed round the room,
Leaping skywards to the sound
Of songs from Brigadoon,
There was no sign of slow decline from
Mrs Ravoon!

211.

So many close shaves and narrow escapes
From disease to the scaffold in Troon,
Surviving space, and leprosy
And the bugs of Cameroon,
Yet one small bag of poppy-sap
From the markets of Kowloon
Could warm the freeze, yet bring to her knees, the addict:
Mrs Ravoon!

212.

In a jar in the sweetshop
In downtown Dunoon,
One leftover jelly
Was slowly turning broon,
Silently evolving
Into a cocoon,
Which contained a strange mutation of
Mrs Ravoon!

213.
She had a baby she sold to buy drugs
To a slave trader based in Kowloon
Now she subsists on spiders and slugs
Which she shares with a handsome dragoon,
She sits in her cave just a tapping her feet
As she listens to Bing Crosby croon
Any semblance of taste is soon laid to waste, in the company of
Mrs Ravoon!

214.
Nothing had prepared the world
For the occurrences post-monsoon,
When something crawled out of the sweetshop
That rainswept afternoon,
Part-jelly, part arachnid
Another part huboon,
It slowly slithered toward the cave, searching for
Mrs Ravoon!

215.
With tentacles madly waving away
Some grit picked up from a dune,
Making its way 'cross the stinking beach
That bordered the stagnant lagoon,
A curious creature headed along
The path twixt the cave and Dunoon,
As it desperately sought the company of its mother:
Mrs Ravoon!

216.

Winding along a treacherous pathway
Subsisting on sips of matzoon,
The jelly-like substance observed in the distance
A cavemouth lit up by the moon,
It gave a small shiver, its nostrils aquiver
To a stink like an unwashed racoon,
At the end of its journey, there on a gurney, prostrate lay
Mrs Ravoon!

217.

Gazing out of the cavemouth
With eyes like slits at noon,
Recalling adventures far to the south
In the jungles of Cancun,
Where through impenetrable mist
She'd spied that young dragoon,
Nostalgia made a sorry state of a horrified
Mrs Ravoon![11]

218.

When a baby needs its mother
Even one that's a loon,
Heaven and earth will not keep them apart
And that can be quite a boon,
But sometimes things can go awry
So beware the silver spoon
That at first seems trusty, yet soon turns rusty when proffered by
Mrs Ravoon!

---

11 Edited, the edit credited to Liz Elliot

219.

Twigs and stones and bracken
Along the pathway strewn,
Caused its pace to slacken
On the journey through Dunoon,
Its small heart had been shaken;
A throbbing pit within a prune,
Sobbing, hoping to awaken some small spark in
Mrs Ravoon!

220.

Venomously cursing as she awoke
And spitting cruel words at the moon,
Joyless and barren her body bespoke
Of tedium, meanness and gloom,
There was scant hope at the end of that rope
Which bound her to life, and had shewn
That hell-for-leather nothing could tether the heartstrings of
Mrs Ravoon!

221.

Onward it trudged through the darkness
Braving icicles sleet and typhoon,
Its progress impeded at every step
As if drawn in a nightmare cartoon,
But nothing could stop it from reaching
Its goal, neither God nor gaboon,
And there'd be no rest till it put to the test the mettle of
Mrs Ravoon!

222.

As a whirlpool of pestilence
Disturbed the bleak lagoon,
Microbes and bacteria
Descended on Dunoon,
While a creature made of jelly
Sought its mother's love and soon
The hand that was offered silently proffered a spider for
Mrs Ravoon!

223.

Waving arms like tentacles
And screaming like a loon,
Aiming venom with precision
Sharp as her harpoon,
Angered by the loathsome thing
That slithered 'cross the dune,
Maternal feelings held no sway over
Mrs Ravoon!

224.

By the dawn's early light
At the fall of the moon,
On the crest of the hill
Overlooking Dunoon,
A lone figure cried out
In grave misfortune,
As the townspeople gazed up at
Mrs Ravoon!

225.
Unhinged by the sight of her child
Who'd appeared as if from a cocoon,
At the cavemouth two weeks before
With jelly-like skin, deep maroon,
She had rended her hair and emoted
Like no time since her days in Kowloon,
Wholesale confusion, like nuclear fusion, unsettled
Mrs Ravoon!

226.
The state of the child was horrendous,
Blobs of jelly around it were strewn,
The stench it emitted, tremendous
Like the anal glands of a racoon,
With outstretched arms it had gestured
In the style of an angry baboon,
Which first gave a start, and then touched the heart, of the
tormented
Mrs Ravoon!

227.
Volcanic emotions threatened to erupt
And spew lava into the lagoon,
Conflicted confusion, unseen and abrupt,
Mocked the sunlight that pale afternoon,
None but a goatherd had seen such despair
Yet he had been drowned in Rangoon,
By malevolent fingers which tore out the hair, of the much rattled
Mrs Ravoon!

227a. (New Year Pome)

At one minute to midnight
All through Dunoon,
Bagpipes were blaring
A hideous tune,
Deafening all those
Who would seek to impugn,
Or otherwise insult
The resident loon.
Who sat in her cave
By the light of the moon,
Munching on spiders
She'd caught by the dune,
Rising up from the edge
Of the stagnant lagoon,
While patiently grooming
A vicious baboon,
With a glint in its eye
Which hinted that soon
There'd be fresh hell and turmoil, from
Mrs Ravoon!

228.

The crowd all went bananas
As they waved at the balloon,
Which sailed through the clear blue sky
Above the rank lagoon,
Could it be a stranger
Come to visit old Dunoon?
Or was it something more malign, like
Mrs Ravoon!?

229.

The apple of her eye was a baby made of jelly
With a look about it somewhat like a loon,
With malformed limbs, a single eye, some scabs and somewhat
smelly
Yet it brightened up her entire afternoon,
But when it came to night-time and the sun began to fall
The baby's one eye fixed upon the moon,
And it commenced to howling, it just wouldn't stop at all, which
exasperated
Mrs Ravoon!

230.

Walking o'er the water
By means of the pontoon,
She gazed at the horizon
Where she'd form a new commune,
If she could motivate the crowd
At a moment opportune
There'd be no limit to the rise, of
Mrs Ravoon!

231.

A bonfire on the mountainside
Lit up all Dunoon,
The celebratory fireworks
Could be seen as far as Troon,
But these solo celebrations
Were all over fairly soon:
As along the Firth they mourned the birth, of
Mrs Ravoon!

232.

The day that followed the beginning of time
Had an overcast afternoon,
The sun went in leaving only a mist
Which enshrouded the putrid lagoon,
From the depths came a gas which rose as a bubble
Weird patterns emerged in a plume,
Taking formative shape and portending trouble, was the primeval
Mrs Ravoon!

233.

When the Mayflower set sail for the New World
They thought it would be such a boon,
Everything there would be better
The future could not come too soon,
But along with the smallpox and bibles
A malignancy straight from the tomb,
Was carried unwitting there with them—the stowaway
Mrs Ravoon!

234.

Halfway across the atlantic
Was a shark with a head like a spoon,
No hammerhead this, there was something amiss
Its whole body was like a cartoon,
The ship's captain tried to pursue it
And bring it down with his harpoon,
But the one to prevail, and make it turn tail, was scary old
Mrs Ravoon!

The Last Judgement (detail): Jan van Eyck

235.

On the Web a debate has been raging
On the subject of where verse is hewn,
Does it spring fully formed from a poet now ageing?
Do wild words need a provident prune?
Could there be any truth that it comes from a tooth—
Does a hole there hold words yet unshewn?
Or, as once admitted, are they transmitted, like brain-waves by
Mrs Ravoon!?

236.

With gestures wild she hurled her child
Up high as if to the moon,
And in a flash with a watery splash
To the bed of the sea it went doon,
The very air crackled—demented she cackled
Staggering from the pontoon,
Inside her a stone, raw ice and cold bone formed the essence of
Mrs Ravoon!

237.

Under the waves in the dark icy deep
In the watery home of Neptune,
Surrounded by fish, and fronds that go swish
Lies a baby once pink but now broon,
Nibbled by crabs and covered in scabs
It may one day wash up on the dune,
Its small body will tell, with a terrible smell, of the cruelty of
Mrs Ravoon![12]

12 YIKES—What a horrible pome, sorry!

238.

Discovered by the captain the stowaway was cast
From the ship to live the life of a maroon,
Solitude and hunger were her lot until at last
A companion was washed up in a typhoon,
Yet friendship was impossible, and loneliness endured
All empathy bound up in a cocoon,
There was little human feeling and no use in appealing, to the
misanthropic
Mrs Ravoon!

239.

Howling resounding, the mountains were bleak
But for that all lay still 'neath the moon,
In the town all was dark but a glimmer did leak
From a candle as froth from the spume,
Flickering weakly and blasted by wind
What small heat it gave vanished too soon,
To warm up the bones, and diminish the moans, of the shivering
Mrs Ravoon!

240.

In the depths of the cave
She scratched with a spoon,
A gruel made of porridge
And spiders, and prune,
And wee droplets of vinegar
Which she'd consume,
The decrepit, ascetic,
Mrs Ravoon!

241.

Gibbering lustily, dancing a jig
To the strains of an old threadbare tune,
Played on some bagpipes made from a pig
That she'd slaughtered that same afternoon,
In the bright of the day she appeared almost gay,
Round her ankles small flowers lay strewn,
There was no second guessing, no future in messing, with the
    capering
Mrs Ravoon!

242.

On a whim, she'd spread a banquet out
Above the vile lagoon,
The cave all swept, a sign she'd kept
Read *Mrs R!'s Saloon,*
A hundred invitations sent;
What would the guests consume?
Opinion divided—the stew provided was made by
Mrs Ravoon!

243.

The ingredients and the sauces of the many courses
Served and eaten that fine afternoon,
Caused many there to wonder if they'd made a blunder
In accepting hospitality too soon,
There was something not quite right, and by night a ghastly blight
Afflicted all the people of Dunoon,
Through evening's gathering mists, many shook their fists at the
    cackling hostess
Mrs Ravoon!

244.

Rumours of jollity spread through the land,
The townsfolk all thought her a loon;
They'd long had misgivings, and once they had planned
To ship her straight back to Rangoon.
Venom and misery they understood;
Traits that they'd gladly impugn,
But her joyous abandon bespake nothing good,
To the neighbours of
Mrs Ravoon!

245.

What was the secret kept hid by the mask?
Had some ill wind now changed the fortune,
Of the poisonous woman oft' taken to task
For the black cloud that shadowed Dunoon?
Small rays of sunshine now seemed to break through,
Yet to cheerfulness most were immune,
Nervous vexation took seed and soon grew
'Gainst the sea-change in
Mrs Ravoon!

246.

She swept as a hurricane down from the cave,
Like some pestilent toxic typhoon;
Maniacal laughter as grim as the grave
Filled the air like a mordant monsoon.
Windows were shuttered, great bolts sealed the doors,
Messrs Campbell, McKay, and McClune
Gathered up rifles, pikes and Claymores
And aimed them at
Mrs Ravoon!

247.

The high street, deserted, through curtains they peered
At the figure that rose from the dune,
The bravest of men tore out great chunks of beard
The most stoical ladies did swoon;
They watched it approach, and then pass and then stop
By the doorway beside the saloon,
Then with a wild hop, into the sweet shop
Strode the mesmerised
Mrs Ravoon!

248,

In the first bloom of youth she'd had a sweet tooth
And a penchant for a macaroon,
But the passage of time, causing dental decline,
Made her masticate like some baboon.
Now when she succumbs she uses her gums,
A dribble of sweetness runs doon
Her stubbly chin, much to the chagrin
Of the sticky faced
Mrs Ravoon!

248a.

She went into the gift-shoppe looking for a curiosity;
The finest shoppe of its kind in Dunoon.
But next door, in the tea-rooms, she committed an atrocity
By gobbling down their every macaroon.
When presented with the bill, she left the shoppe at great velocity;
They chased her down the hill and very soon,
Word spread far and wide about this greedy old monstrosity,
A sign went up: *KEEP OUT,*
Mrs Ravoon![13]

13 In honour of the gift shop and tea rooms, with thanks to Stewart Bell for the photos from Dunoon.

249.

Butterscotch and humbugs, pastilles, Victory V's,
Were all lined up in jars around the room;
Acid drops and dolly mixture, sherbet, treats, all these
She'd hastily and lustily subsume
Into a sickly gobstopper which held her in its thrall,
Seeming bigger than the distant marbled moon,
The sugary contents of this haul, demanding several pints of gall
Were guzzled by the mute
Mrs Ravoon!

250.

Her neck was high-tensile, her coccyx prehensile,
Her odour much like a racoon.
There was no use denying, that though she'd been trying
Her manners were of a baboon.
Despite her new dress, which she'd bought to impress
A young, suave, and charming dragoon,
No miraculous saviour could curb her behaviour
Or civilise
Mrs Ravoon!

251.

Tempting him with bags of sweets up to her lonely cave,
Her lust was focussed on the suave dragoon.
Little did he know that he was destined for a grave
Which already held the goatherd from Kowloon.
As he innocently followed, not a second thought he gave
To his perilous position, until soon
In unnatural postures, he was probed until he craved
Death's sweet release, from
Mrs Ravoon!

252.
Smashing up her pottery and storming from the scene,
Screams of fury told of misfortune;
Despite winning the lottery her face turned violent green,
Her lucky numbers proving picayune.
By the cave a thorny thicket of gorse shredded the ticket,
There were ragged bits of paper widely strewn,
Now voided for selection, there were wails of disaffection
From the anguished and distraught
Mrs Ravoon!

253.
Munching on a long-pig served with kidney beans and rice
At a cafe in the back streets of Kowloon;
Determined not to miss the chance of sampling every vice,
She scooped up fresh-cooked entrails with a spoon,
Which she would later use to cook some newly purchased drugs
After first becoming loaded on majoun.
Lying semi-conscious in the shadows, gnawed by bugs,
In the arms of morphia, lay
Mrs Ravoon!

254.
Torpid in her reverie, mad dreams came fast and loose,
As she lay in thankless gutters 'neath the moon.
Bolstered by the painless calming balm of poppy-juice,
Her sinuous fingers clutched the rusty spoon.
Memories of times spent munching spiders in her cave
Brought a twinge of sweet nostalgia for Dunoon,
Her condition was precarious, she was the needles slave:
That opiated shell,
Mrs Ravoon!

Fumatrici di Oppio: Gaetano Previati

254.
Her hungers were insatiable, her appetites extreme;
Satisfaction hard to gain, and like a loon,
She sought out all sensation, until every vice would seem
Just a single drop of rain in a monsoon.
Her pursuits were inconclusive, her goals remained elusive,
Cravings came at times inopportune;
Every course of action was an unwanted distraction
Serving only to displease
Mrs Ravoon!

255.
Gathering her thoughts like leaves thrust deep into a bag,
She had formed a strange and mystical commune;
Suppressing wild impulses which only served to drag
Her into an existence garbage-strewn,
A steely eyed resolve to end the conflict and the strife
Came upon her as she pondered; maybe soon
Some stranger might appear who'd try to make an honest wife
Of the malevolent old hag,
Mrs Ravoon!

256.
A young man in a turban sat in silence sipping bourbon,
In the hot and steamy humid afternoon.
A stranger in the bar, he had travelled from afar,
To seek the truth in rumours spoken of Kowloon.
He had heard the place was swimming, with wild and willing women,
And he had no inkling of the misfortune
Which he would soon encounter, when he tried to mount a
Very keen but deeply mean
Mrs Ravoon!

257.

From the darkness came the sounds of grunting, and the smell of sweat,
Something rancid mixed with passion's sweet perfume;
The air was thick as honey and the bed was soaking wet,
Greasy droplets glazed the windows of the room.
There was something most unnerving, yet too late to think of swerving
From the climax of the night, arriving soon,
Though the outlook was distasteful, he thought it would be wasteful
Not to try to satisfy
Mrs Ravoon!

258.

The young man seemed so innocent, his blushing cheeks so fair,
The down upon his face a dusky broon,
He had not a penny spent, she gently brushed his hair,
Her curious odour nearly made him swoon.
The wondrous things she proffered seemed to come without a price
Yet the rings she gave were not gold, but jargoon.
When he offered of himself she took, not once or twice but thrice
Yet it failed to satisfy
Mrs Ravoon!

259.

Disappointed in her dalliance and feeling in a mood,
She left the bed and wandered from the room,
Completely unaware that her behaviour might seem rude;
From pangs of conscience she was quite immune.
She'd known for years that nobody would want her for a wife,
And decided to return to the commune,
Then in silence she despatched her sleeping lover with a knife;
An act which satisfied
Mrs Ravoon!

260.

Inside the gated compound, confusion seemed to reign;
The communards all hummed a dismal tune,
Their guru seemed to thrive upon their existential pain
And forced them to wear sackcloth, roughly hewn.
Down in hidden dungeons, fetid air was hard to breathe,
For those inclined to forsake the commune;
Who found themselves in chains—it was impossible to leave,
For their unlikely guru was,
Mrs Ravoon![14]

261.[15]

Enslaved by cruel addictions, pressed down by unknown forces,
Once young skin now wrinkled like a prune,
Strange hungers captivated her and pulled like wild horses,
Stabbing at her soul like a harpoon,
Endless avenues of emptiness, cold vistas of the void,
Stretched out before her, threatening to consume;
The only pleasure left to her was found in schadenfreude
Which brought cold comfort to
Mrs Ravoon!

262.

Strapping a grenade to a newly rescued cat
And pointing it toward the closed commune,
She covered up her ears then she rearranged her hat,
And waited keenly for the coming boom.
Bricks and mortar, dirt and dust, bits of fur and gore
Fell through the sky; the cat now widely strewn,
She turned her back on the attack, walked off, and furthermore
No clue would implicate
Mrs Ravoon![16]

14 Boom, tish...
15 Ravoon 261–285 (before the computer explosion).
16 Thanks to Mike Hardaker for the recent illustration of a suicide cat.

263.

The temple lay in ruins, there was nothing left but rubble,
Sacred artefacts lay widely strewn.
The future seemed uncertain with forebodings of trouble;
It would take her several moments to attune
To all the possibilities destruction seemed to bring;
Like an idyll in the eye of a typhoon,
As trepidation disappeared and uncertainty took wing
An icy calmness soon infused
Mrs Ravoon!

264.

Bored with her existence, in search of new beginnings
She walked into a bookies in Kowloon,
Where she gambled all the commune's money, won, and with the winnings
Bought a ticket on a boat bound for Dunoon.
Her heart set on the slender comforts waiting in her cave,
Where slugs and spiders dwelt in putrid gloom;
She imagined she'd find welcome there, but nobody forgave
The past transgressions of
Mrs Ravoon!

265.

Everybody's heard about old habits dying hard,
From Australia across to old Cancun;
But even a degenerate can cling on to a shard
Of hope that some transcendence may come soon.
Some may wring their hands in desperation, or might pray
Their sins would wash away in a monsoon,
While others are more sanguine, and contentedly they stay
Immersed in mischief, like
Mrs Ravoon!

266.
In the temple she had grafted on some insect DNA
Which, to her, all things considered, was a boon;
She hoped that she'd be spinning webs of steely silken grey,
Would be scaling walls and catching flies quite soon.
Although she might look somewhat odd with six more pairs of eyes,
And now and then producing a cocoon,
Nothing now could stop her seeking out her cherished prize—
Global terror of
Mrs Ravoon!

267.
Despite deluded fantasies of global domination,
In solitude she lived by the lagoon.
Spending time with other people merely brought frustration
As most of them just saw her as a goon.
In time, she pondered, "Could it be that all this isolation
Will do its worst, or render me immune
To the arrows and the slings that my lonely lifestyle brings?"
Thus ran the thoughts that fraught
Mrs Ravoon!

268.
Her hybrid self fixated on the walls around the cave,
From the ceiling stalactites were hanging doon.
Seeking out the darkest corners, silent as the grave,
She hovered watchfully over Dunoon.
Hanging from a new-spun web, malevolent and cruel,
Reassured her pangs of hunger would quite soon
Be satisfied by slurping down a bowl of human gruel;
A baleful hiss came from
Mrs Ravoon!

269.
A peculiar kind of energy was coursing through her veins
Like a wolf might feel when howling at full moon.
In need of food she contemplated seeking out some brains
To pour into her casseroled cardoon.
So putting on a Stetson, and reaching for her gun,
She slowly made her way into Dunoon
Where, engaged in violent mayhem only she considered fun,
A ghoulish craving filled
Mrs Ravoon!

270.
As springtime turned to summer, and the rising sun grew bright,
She lightly danced across the sandy dune,
And walked above the sparkling water bathing in the light
Reflecting through the slats of the pontoon.
A crispness in the air betrayed the northern latitude,
Disguising putrid smells from the lagoon;
A gentle breeze just served to tease a brand new attitude
From an upbeat, born again,
Mrs Ravoon!

271.
Quite fetching in a newly-made and flowing floral dress
Of primrose yellow fashioned from cantoon,
Nobody suspected, indeed none would ever guess
Her secrets, nor would they seek to impugn
The character of such a vision, lovely in the light,
As buoyant as a helium balloon;
But after dark came a revision: deep in inky night
Depravity transformed
Mrs Ravoon!

272.

In the morning she would wash her face, and gaily plait her hair,
Around her neck sweet garlands she'd festoon;
To look at her it seemed as if she didn't have a care,
Or give a heck for knowing her fortune.
But once the sun had fallen and cold darkness filled the sky,
Maleficent misdeeds beneath the moon
Took up her time, absorbed her mind, and if you asked her why,
She'd scowl and say, "Coz I'm
Mrs Ravoon!"

273.

It isn't every day you get a visit
From someone who's come all the way from Troon
But then it isn't very likely somehow, is it,
If that someone had been born with silver spoon
While you were left in poverty and hunger,
Munching insects while they courted a tycoon?
Destiny had smiled upon the younger
Sister, not on poor
Mrs Ravoon!

274.

Obsessed with sibling rivalry, itching for a fight
And fashioning a weapon from a spoon,
She rounded on her relative—she'd been awake all night
Making gruesome offerings to the moon.
Leaping in a frenzy and half crazed from drinking gin,
Screaming vile insults like a loon,
It was not quite clear at this point which sister might win;
The younger one, or old
Mrs Ravoon!

275.

Blood was spurting everywhere, the cavern floor was slick,
The once grey rocks around were turned maroon.
A battle was ensuing, it was ratchet versus stick,
Hair was pulled and flesh from bone was hewn.
Heads were bashed as sisters clashed and, tangled, span around,
One tripped, one slipped, a yell, one fell, and soon
The younger sister smote a throat until a gurgling sound
Escaped the windpipe of
Mrs Ravoon!

276.

Bleeding from the throat, and scuttling sideways like a crab,
She headed for the banks of the lagoon;
But not before she lunged once more and with a brutal stab
Impaled her sister on the sharpened spoon.
Knowing that before the dawn she'd need to clear the scene
She dragged the body out on the pontoon,
And soon the bloodsoaked corpse was sinking, 'neath the waters green,
And calm descended on
Mrs Ravoon!

277.

A certain kind of feeling can be difficult to get,
When emotionally one is out of tune.
But in moments of high tragedy a fleeting small regret
Might pass across one usually immune
To sentiments quite normal at the passing of one's sister;
Her body now interred in the lagoon,
Yet generally she thought of her as no more than a blister:
Popped, then forgotten, by
Mrs Ravoon!

278.

Infection soon set in, and the slices in her neck
Turned gangrenous, emitting a perfume
Vile and putrid, fetid, foul; her body was a wreck,
Her time was running short, she knew that soon
Assistance would be needed, so she swiftly made her way
To a nursing home in Manningford Bohune,
Where mute nurses carefully tended, and ended the decay
That had threatened to engulf
Mrs Ravoon![17]

279.

Her sister's husband was quite dull; a small and portly man,
Who unexpectedly arrived from Brigadoon.
"Where's my wife?" he bravely asked, but very shortly ran,
Escaping 'cross the mountainside till soon
From up above there came a sound, a screaming rent his ears,
Emanating from a small hot air balloon.
Plutonium and missiles fell on him like burning tears
Dropped by his nemesis
Mrs Ravoon!

280.

While looking down from up above, and relishing the scene
Of desolation that surrounded the lagoon,
The tiny specks of human flesh, all around, had been
Much like minute motes of blood in a spittoon.
Her sister's husband's balding head, his feet, his ears and nose,
Now separated, had been widely strewn.
At the bottom of a crater, in a place where nothing grows,
Contemplating, sits
Mrs Ravoon!

---

17 Thanks to Mike Hardaker for the location of the nursing home.

281.
After the catastrophe the sky turned dark and grim,
Nobody could even see the moon.
Radiation brought confusion—were they fish, fowl, her or him?
Was apocalypse just shorthand for High Noon?
With most people incinerated to an ashen mound;
Calamity, that hateful hermit's tune;
The silence, so profound, served only to astound
The sole survivor, one
Mrs Ravoon!

282.
Starting out on burgundy, she was the toast of France,
That warm night with a handsome octaroon,
When frenzied music in the air caused everyone to dance
To melodies played on a wild bassoon.
The merry airs, the lack of cares, the mad desire to prance,
Absinthe heated up in a teaspoon,
Diverted all attention, therefore no-one looked askance,
At the stark-naked and drunk
Mrs Ravoon!

283.
Reclining in a beach chair on the sunny riviera,
Drinking kir mixed with the pulp of prune,
Without a care although her hair, now grey, had once been fairer
And her many wrinkles showed through her costume,
She flirted with the *maitre d'* who hovered o'er the pebbles
Bearing little plates of morsels to consume.
Though at one amongst the jet-set she was more at home with rebels,
And a cunning plan hatched in
Mrs Ravoon!

284.

Fresh from the casino where her luck had not been good,
Befriended by a highly trained baboon,
A calculated plot was born which ultimately could
Result in either failure or fortune.
While all the guests were dining out, or basking on the beach,
The two of them would ransack every room,
And quickly but still carefully steal everything in reach;
The shiftless simian, and
Mrs Ravoon!

285.

Engrossed with acquisition, and consumed by guiltless greed,
Silently she stole through every room;
Lusting after trinkets which she didn't really need,
She dreamt she might turn into a tycoon.
If she could just accumulate enormous mounds of cash
(Which, naturally she'd share with the baboon),
And, with stealth, gain wealth judiciously, without being too rash
Which was never easy for
Mrs Ravoon![18]

18 On the occasion of losing a number of (as yet unpublished/ un-posted) Pomes due to my computer exploding, several people wrote their own pomes to commiserate, and express their hopes that Mrs R! would not be gone for long… this was by way of a reply from me:

An Other Pome, by Anne Other.

I could have got depressed, but instead I've been surprised
By Pomes that have risen from the crew,
Feelings long suppressed are not, as once surmised,
Like gnomes left out for too long in the dew.
They are not damp or soggy, they do not smell of mould,
Their little hats are merry, not dark blue,
And therefore like a troglodyte

286.

A sack of stolen diamonds was taken to a *fence*
In Paris, where he used a *nom de plume;*
For every hundred Euros worth, he offered fifty pence,
Which enraged the thieves, especially the baboon,
Who'd imagined a retirement filled with leisure and recline
In a self-designed, luxurious, saloon;
But the timely want of opium, in preference to wine,
Made the deal appeal to
Mrs Ravoon!

287.

Sleepless nights were spent beneath a bridge beside the Seine,
Where she shivered through the dawn till after noon.
It was obvious to anyone with even half a brain;
Her proclivities had caused her ill fortune.
If she could find a remedy to curb her bad behaviour,
She might reverse the curse portending doom;
Perhaps salvation might be sought, and found, in Scandinavia?
So onward trekked the wrecked
Mrs Ravoon!

Unused to the bright daylight
I'll say not Adios, nor bid Adieu;
But hope that with the rising sun,
Another pome will be done,
And sent from Mrs R! direct to you.

As the hernia said to the truss—thanks for the support!

288.

Trudging 'cross the tundra, sliced by snow and wracked by ice,
Her shadow slid beneath a heartless moon.
Hounded by haunting memories of every kind of vice,
She sought refuge in Ygdrassil, writ in rune,
In whose branches dwelt a dragon, eagles, stags, and several more
With whose presence she attempted to attune.
Swigging from a flagon, she raised defiant fists at Thor;
That challenger of Gods,
Mrs Ravoon!

289.

Abandoning the reindeer, and the chariot she'd rode in,
Which was now concealed inside an icy tomb,
Her fight with Thor had caused a thaw; for an encore she fought
Odin;
A clash which caused a flash as if the moon
Had splintered like the sunlight, now reflecting from the snow,
Much like diamonds spilt from split rocks, freshly hewn.
She found a liking for the Viking everyone would shortly know,
As the inner spirit of
Mrs Ravoon!

290.

Adorned with horned helmet, like a beetle or a stag;
Lost in wastelands, swigging bottles of DeKroon;
Eating lichen, moss, and bitter herbs she kept in a bag
She had fashioned with a festive gay galloon;
Raging 'gainst the elements, invoking Ragnarok,
Hoping against hope that time would soon
Cease endlessly unrolling, indifferent, as to mock
The entire existence of
Mrs Ravoon!

291.

Drinking pints of reindeer blood inside a shed of snow,
And pondering the strife of poor fortune,
Ice-cold crunchy spiders were her lunch today, but no—
She'd rather be the wife of some Walloon!
A life of constant struggle made her long for some relief
And an effort must be made to find it soon;
Was it too late for her to turn over a new leaf?
A moral crisis faced
Mrs Ravoon!

292.

In solitude she faced her demons, wondering if fate
Would find her fading 'neath the icy moon,
Or if one final fatal effort might exterminate
That which plagued her, like some lost platoon
Of ghastly ghostly memories lined up into her past;
Forgotten nightmares she feared to exhume;
A cataclysmic blast might set her free, at last,
And liberate loathsome
Mrs Ravoon!

293.

Northward bound she somehow found herself feasting upon meat
Piled high on oak slabbed tables, roughly hewn;
There were legs and drumsticks, torsos, heads, elbows, breast and feet,
She gorged herself from midnight through till noon.
Her ribcage ached; no candied cake could make her feel replete,
With gruesome groans, still tossing bones, her belly a balloon,
Her gore smeared body cracked her seat;
Finally floored, resounding snores, came from
Mrs Ravoon!

294.[19]

Deep in psychosis she slept in the snow
As icicles fell from the moon,
Dripping upon her as dawns early glow
Brought inklings of warmth, but so soon
Darkness came back, the day all too brief,
So far north it was black before noon
The months passed by slowly, and brought no relief
To the chilled bones of
Mrs Ravoon!

295.

Surviving on puffins and reindeer blood
Scooped up with an old rusty spoon,
Her face smeared with penguin gore, arms caked in mud,
She hacked at the ice like a loon.
Cackling to no-one "I may be some time,"
As she hummed a delusional tune;
No reason or rhyme could wipe clean the grime
Stained conscience of
Mrs Ravoon!

---

19 Post Psychosis Blues...
We left her a few weeks ago in Scandinavia gorging on meat... now she has headed further north, and it is very cold...

296.

Bewildered by magnetism, at the wrong pole
And thinking of Scott, not DeKroon,
Gulping down wildlife which she swallowed whole
She was finding it hard to attune
To the wastes of the north, which she took for south,
With scant guidance from stars in the gloom;
The raw penguin meat, which she gummed with her mouth?
Phantoms conjured by
Mrs Ravoon!

297.

A blizzard obscured the far distant tent
She had left in despair, until soon,
Her footprints were gone; which direction she went
Made no difference, each pathway bestrewn
With grey frozen rocks that all looked the same
As her eyesight grew dim and immune
To changes in light, 'twas the end of the game
For the frostbitten
Mrs Ravoon!

298.

Convulsions of delirium took deleterious toll,
The days passed by swift, in a swoon.
Propulsion spasmodic, the depths of her soul
Cried out for relief, and yet soon
She began to believe she would never return
To her comfortable cave in Dunoon,
Though she was well travelled she slowly unravelled;
Mad visons plagued
Mrs Ravoon!

299.

Attacking a polar bear, shrieking in glee,
Gore spattered, she formed a harpoon,
From the bones left behind, and half out of her mind,
Each mouthful of fur was a boon.
Red drops in the snow showed the trail left behind
As onward she pushed; Daniel Boone
Though as strong as a tree, was never as free
As the blood-sated
Mrs Ravoon!

300.

With the whiteness all round and the absence of sound,
Apparitions appeared in the gloom.
Her dire condition, devoid of nutrition,
Save the morsels of meat she'd festoon
Around her thin neck as frail as a bird,
Which she'd peck while she dreamed of Dunoon,
She gibbered and wondered, who was the third?
That walked beside
Mrs Ravoon!

301.

Visions of Yggdrasil passed through her fevered brain.
Ragnarok could hardly come too soon.
Clawing over ice floes that drove her quite insane
As her thoughts turned to her home by the lagoon.
Just then her eyes set on a solitary boat,
Rowing past her far beneath a crescent moon;
Her shrieks becoming frantic, she was soon on the Atlantic.
And the ice receded from
Mrs Ravoon!

302.

'Twas thanks to Mary Shelley, who with cunning, style, and guile,
Created the kind rescuer—a boon!
Though Mrs R! was smelly, soon they passed a Faroe Isle
Where whales' blood swiftly turned the sea maroon.
In former days, imagining that she would surely starve,
She'd cursed the gods, whose wisdom she'd impugn.
But now the silent monster drew a knife and slowly carved
A lump of blubber for
Mrs Ravoon!

303.

Nostrils twitching in delight at the stench of the blood,
She emitted a hideous croon.
Whales whose memories stretched back to the flood,
Lay slaughtered and breached, bleached bones strewn
Across the sands, as gore-stained hands
Mixed fish-flesh with stewed wild cardoon;
The Faroe festival in frightful flight,
Whet the appetite of
Mrs Ravoon!

304.

Ruefully recalling all the chances she had missed,
Like the time she lost her heart to a dragoon,
Whose eyes shone out like diamonds, and whose cold lips she had kissed,
With a tenderness that now seemed out of tune
With a mis-spent life of dissipation,
Cruelty, and bestrewn
With unpaid loans, broken bones, a future of damnation;
Too late, regret beset
Mrs Ravoon!

305.

Turning to the monstrous one who rowed her boat ashore,
She asked him if he thought she was a loon?
The Creature looked up sorrowfully, sighed, but said no more;
She began to think their feelings were in tune,
For she was full of self-reflection, weariness, and doubt,
While he had clearly suffered misfortune,
Could this being be the one she could not live without?
A small light glowed inside
Mrs Ravoon!

306.

Onward she impelled her frame
Determined not to prune,
These newly growing buds, so game,
Bursting out like June.
She turned her face toward the west,
To quell the wild typhoon,
Of confusion pounding in her chest,
Which thrilled
Mrs Ravoon!

307.

She took the Creature by its hand
And led him 'neath the shadow of a dune.
Laying down, her passions fanned,
Like flames as she inhaled his strange perfume.
The waves rolled in around them,
And, impaled, she yelled out, "Do not stop so soon."
But he fell limp, and like a gimp.
Spent, he staggered from
Mrs Ravoon!

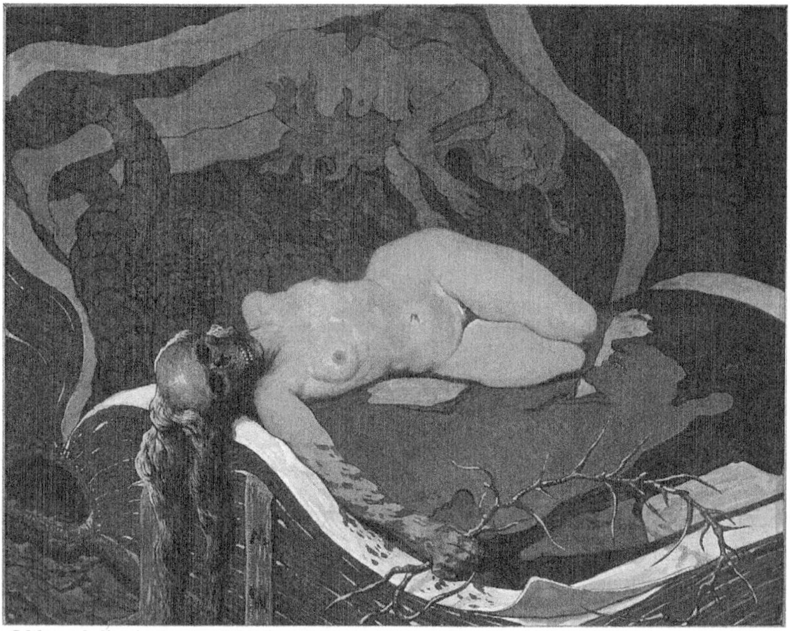

Old truth lies in books: Marian Wawrzeniecki

308.

Frustrated and in highest heat,
Her passion turned too soon,
To volcanic rage, complete
With forebodings of doom.
She bound the Creature to a stake,
Affixed a tight bradoon,
And led it back, tied in a sack, to slake
Mrs Ravoon!

309.

When aroused and in full spate, and pent-up passions profligate;
She would willingly lay down with a racoon.
Disappointment hit her hard, and marred her dalliance with fate;
The Creature, come so late, had come too soon.
It was clear he could not feed her need, and she would never beg,
Nor play the part of some artless buffoon;
Notions in her head took seed, she swore to take him down a peg
As onanism freed
Mrs Ravoon!

310.

Back in the boat, and still remote, from any place she'd wish,
She wondered at the vagaries of fortune;
Then deftly threw a rope that snagged a speedy passing fish,
Which pulled them 'cross the oceans to Gombroon.
'Twas there she'd slain a prior love,
A goatherd she had drowned in the Karun.
Beware the iron-fisted velvet glove,
Worn by
Mrs Ravoon!

311.

Strolling gaily through the streets, clad in a silken gown,
Edged with cuffs of finely wrought gadroon,
With one eye on the Creature and one on Persian brown,
Some form of satisfaction would come soon.
Whether found in stupefaction, or in satiated lust,
It was clear that by the rising of the moon,
Surprising new developments would come, which surely must
Restore good temper to
Mrs Ravoon!

312.

Haggling at a market stall with her new-found connection,
Fingers trembling as she rubbed her trusty spoon,
A price was fixed and thus she nixed prior thoughts of vivisection,
And reached into her purse for a doubloon.
But what was this? Where had it gone? Deep inside her pocket
Was a hole, the coin had rolled, and like a loon
She gnashed and wailed, her ship had sailed, she went off like a
rocket;
A wave of rage engulfed
Mrs Ravoon!

313.

The Creature stood by, mortified, unsure how to react;
Some course of action must be taken soon.
His stoic nature petrified as she seemed to enact
The very essence of a wild typhoon.
Blasting out from every pore a ceaseless stream of fury,
As she lost all hope of opium or majoun,
He could not budge, nor would he judge; there was no mortal jury
To perceive what guilt lay in
Mrs Ravoon!

314.

The tides of time rolled in, relentless,
Lapping the lagoon;
For centuries she had lived repentless,
Raging at the moon,
Which, far above her, cast its light
On foul and fair. Now shewn
That every wrong can't be made right,
Doubt dogged
Mrs Ravoon!

315.

Standing in the marketplace, as all around her burned,
The matches she had struck now widely strewn,
She held the Creature's hand, and in her heart she yearned,
For opiates, for love, and for Dunoon.
Deep down inside 'twas all the same, no matter where she
    travelled,
Through icy realms of madness, or monsoon;
In life's cruel game, to remain sane, as her brain unravelled
Was a tightrope trick for poor
Mrs Ravoon!

316.

One hand on the tiller, and one upon the sail,
She steered a stolen boat from the pontoon.
The Creature looked on keenly, his ears pierced by a wail
Emitting from her mouth; a high-pitched croon,
Which shattered all illusions that she was ever able
To hit a note, or hold the simplest tune.
It was luck alone which blocked the coiled cable
Set to strangle and silence
Mrs Ravoon!

317.

From the corner of her beady eye, she spied the errant hand
That, in exasperation, threatened to festoon
A loosely woven noose—an improvised steel band
Around her scrawny neck, till she had threwn
A shrieking fit of an intensity so great
It burst the Creature's pique like a balloon.
Onward they sailed, she loudly wailed; her all but silent mate
Fixated upon
Mrs Ravoon!

318.

Days passed by as balmy breezes pushed them through the water,
They fed on flying fish felled by harpoon.
But nagging doubts crept in, and she felt they really oughta
Pass some other vessel sometime soon.
The Creature gazed adoringly towards her, he was smitten,
His gentle heart turned him into a goon.
At night-time as he nuzzled her, she purred just like a kitten
Which was quite unheard of for
Mrs Ravoon![20]

319.

One morning as the sun rose high a vessel came in sight,
That by night was all but hidden in the gloom.
It came upon them suddenly, and in a fearful fright,
They quickly dressed and put on thick perfume,
In order to appease the crew who seemed intent to fight
The two of them, in case perchance fortune
Be hidden 'neath the decking, but they had not reckoned
On the fiery ire of
Mrs Ravoon!

20 In appeasement of the girlish notions of romance suggested by, ahem, certain readers—make the most of it, as it is very unlikely to recur!

320.

Blows rained down upon their heads;
Spattered blood, maroon,
Lay slick upon the unmade bed
They'd had to leave too soon,
Though badly bruised and battered
By a nasty nailed batoon,
The Creature saved the one that mattered—
His dear
Mrs Ravoon!

321.

"A plague upon these pirates, choice,
We'll send them to their tomb,"
Cried out a vehement female voice,
Both violent and immune
To heartfelt pleas for mercy
As she cut the brigands doon.
Each cutlass slash sent waves of passion
Through
Mrs Ravoon!

324.[21]

Although their wounds were deep and raw, salt-spray worked its magic,
As the sunlight gave way to a glistening moon.
Not a single pirate lived, the massacre, though tragic,
Was quick forgot as rotten men went doon,
Into the dark and icy deep,
To dally with Neptune.
The night was young there'd be no sleep, nor she a single tear would weep;
The Creature's only thought: to keep,
Close to
Mrs Ravoon!

---

21 *Editor's note: pomes 322 and 323 seem never to have existed*

325.

Laying down to rest in the bowels of their skiff,
Strange stirrings down below, as they did spoon,
Alarmed the naive Creature, beneath his vest so stiff,
His rigid bones now creaking until soon
Something odd alerted him that all was not quite well,
Frigidity had prior been a boon,
But what was this? A baleful hiss, that steamy, snake-like, fell
From the lips of a lustful
Mrs Ravoon!

326.

She fell upon the Creature and proceeded to undo,
Layers of clothing, which were swiftly strewn,
Around in wild abandon; lost in lust she only knew,
That she must somehow waken this cocoon,
Which surely hid somewhere inside, a butterfly of love,
For her to grasp, the thought fair made her swoon,
But down below, things did not grow, as clouds formed up above,
And foul frustration filled
Mrs Ravoon!

327.

Thundering in anger as her dampness turned to mould,
The snoring Creature now seemed close to doom.
She yelled his name, and pulled his mane; the game grew swiftly old,
And she cursed the carcass of this fleshless goon.
Could he not see the need in her, the act that was his duty?
To serve her deep desires, or to attune?
In sleepy slumber, he remained oblivious to the beauty
Or the burning fires inside
Mrs Ravoon!

Death and the Maiden (detail): Hans Baldung

328.

The dead accursed swine, deep in the icy brine,
Should have brought her joy, like the pashtoon,
She had once despatched with a glass of poisoned wine,
After one long hot impassioned afternoon.
But her mood was somewhat pensive and, unused to reflection,
Her thoughts began to drift to the lagoon;
The Creature, apprehensive, started a collection
Of tiny gifts to please
Mrs Ravoon!

329.

Weighed down with baubles and bangles and beads,
Like some market stall found in Kowloon,
She pondered upon her unsatisfied needs,
Bought off by this flaccid loon.
Were he not so attractive, he'd be long dead,
The parts of his body wide-strewn.
There was something amiss, not quite right in the head, of the
distracted
Mrs Ravoon!

330.

Resting a while on a desert isle
'Neath the banks of a sandy dune,
Her scowl, so foul, gave way to a smile
As she plotted—sometime soon,
To continue their journey home to the cave
On the hillside not far from Dunoon.
A nesting instinct? The Creature was brave
That would go there with
Mrs Ravoon!

331.

They rounded the Cape, surviving on ape
And a small jar of pickled racoon.
Their diet was lean, and made them feel mean
And resentful of sharing a spoon,
Of carefully caught fish, often they'd wish
For some penguin impaled by harpoon,
But their aim was not true, and hunger soon grew
Too much for
Mrs Ravoon!

332.

Begging the Creature to tear off a limb
To stave off her hunger, she soon
Succumbed to her craving, and then began raving,
As wolves do around the full moon.
They both knew the chance of survival was slim,
The very sky seemed to lampoon
Their existence, but meanwhile resistance was futile—
It was thumbs down for
Mrs Ravoon!

333.

Chewing a fingernail not quite her own,
Her jangled nerves played out a tune,
Both un-melodic and so episodic,
A verse took the whole afternoon.
The poor mangled Creature emitted a groan
Like a badly played leaky bassoon.
They rowed their small boat in bouts so spasmodic
That all hope left
Mrs Ravoon!

334.

Drifting on the currents as if on a coffin lid,
Dependent on the mercy of Neptune,
Help came in the form of a massive passing squid,
Whose inky tentacles proved quite a boon.
Pushed by this cephalopod the miles passed by quick,
With the creatures of the ocean, they'd commune;
Raw sardines and seaweed made the Creature somewhat sick,
But more than satisfied
Mrs Ravoon!

335.

Hurtling at a rate of knots they soon left the equator
Far behind them, as the tides turned with the moon.
Racing past the coast of Africa, it was some hours later
That the squid appeared to run out of vavoom;
Then tickling on its tentacles to make it swim some more,
Her heart set on returning to Dunoon,
She fell out of the boat straight into the ocean's maw,
Which soaked and salted poor
Mrs Ravoon!

336 .

Thrashing in the water and cursing as she spat
Out oily brine, she felt like a buffoon.
Nobody had ever taught her and, like a wet cat,
Swimming was an art she'd oft impugn.
Drowning rivals or spent lovers, she could understand,
She would drop them without qualm from the pontoon,
But the simple task of buoyancy was beyond her command,
Which imperilled the once-charmed
Mrs Ravoon!

337.

Reaching for a tentacle she tried hard to get a grip,
But the limb was slimy as an old spittoon;
'Twas impossible to hold on, and she feared to take a trip
To the seabed which was hundreds of leagues doon.
At last she felt a sucker stick itself to her forehead
And lift her in the air—how opportune!
Another minute in the water would have seen her dead;
An undignified end for
Mrs Ravoon!

338.

Although she was safe from the water,
And survival, as such, was a boon,
The mark on her forehead soon taught her,
That gloating can come all too soon.
Though free from concern, and quite glad
To be boating again 'neath the moon,
The weals left behind by the suckery pad
Disfigured
Mrs Ravoon!

339.

Onward they hurtled. 'cross oceans,
Pushed on both by squid and simoon,
In the boat there were some mixed emotions,
Her heart thundered like a typhoon,
As they entered the Clyde, which is tidal,
She adjusted her moist pantaloon,
While her thoughts turned to matters most bridal,
A rare blush coloured
Mrs Ravoon!

340.

In her presence the Creature saw beauty,
Her lank grey hair shone like the moon,
He knew he must soon do his duty
And firmly resolved not to swoon,
At the sight of his mistresses' ankles,
As, around her, used clothing lay strewn,
Fearful, the memory rankles,
That he twice let down
Mrs Ravoon!

341.

She led him by hand up to her homely cave,
On the hillside far above the rank lagoon.
Although he was nervous, he tried hard to be brave
Feeling like an unworthy poltroon.
With a long spindly finger she pointed off afar
To the view overlooking fair Dunoon,
And leaving the cave mouth slightly ajar,
He admired the booty of
Mrs Ravoon!

342.

There were dusty old skulls and half eaten stew,
Cobwebs and such in the room.
It was shadowy, dismal, smelt of mildew,
Yet to him it was almost a womb.
He sank to his knees, helplessly lost
In a reverie, bright in the gloom,
And with heartfelt pleas, said, "No matter what cost,
Please marry me
Mrs Ravoon!"

343.

Her ancient heart pounded and she was aghast;
The Creature had seemed to attune
To her innermost thoughts, could it be, at last
She'd found someone with whom to commune
In domestic bliss, despite her dark past,
Where deceased, murdered, husbands lay strewn?
With a satisfied hiss, the dice were now cast
For the future of
Mrs Ravoon!

344.

It was decided, dates set, she'd said *Yes,*
This had all seemed to happen so soon.
Her forked tongue could find no way to confess
That her rotten heart was all a-swoon.
She tried to stay calm but she was a-flutter,
And danced a crazed jig like a loon,
Yet no sign of alarm and no trace of a stutter
Betrayed poker-faced
Mrs Ravoon!

345.

Guests were invited, a menu was chosen,
A venue booked by the lagoon;
All food must be fresh, with nothing frozen,
She dreamt of a long honeymoon.
The catering came from a lovely new snackbar,
On the backstreets of downtown Dunoon,
Run by a man known only as *Akbar,*[22]
Who had not heard of
Mrs Ravoon!

---

22 *Editor's note: Tim was writing another pome cycle at this point, concerning Akbar's snackbar. Here, the two intersect*

346.

The Kirk had refused them, because they seemed odd,
And said they must wait until June,
But they, in a hurry, were wed on the sod,
Of the hillside above the lagoon,
The bride's dress was sackcloth, the Creature was shod
In boots of a bloody maroon,
They vowed before nature, for there was no God,
That looked kindly 'pon
Mrs Ravoon!

347.

As soon as the wedding was over, the wicked bride's thoughts turned to lust;
She would not wait till their honeymoon,
Wrestling the Creature down into the clover she cried out in passion, "You must
Face your fate and make love to me soon."
She clambered aboard him, her skirts all askew,
And rummaged in his pantaloon.
His face had turned blue; she, ignoring it, knew
Time was ticking for
Mrs Ravoon!

348.

Long bony hands reached around the midriff
Of the Creature laid down on the dune,
Maddened with passion and finding him stiff,
She ached for a single teaspoon
Of his manly elixir; a momentary tiff,
Had come and gone like a typhoon;
The Creature's head reeled as he caught a whiff
Of the newly-wed
Mrs Ravoon!

349.
She lay back in the dewy grass, satisfied and spent,
Listening to the waves on the lagoon
The Creature, newly-wed at last, had both came and went,
Now his visage seemed to wrinkle like a prune,
But when she tried to move him, and tie him to her bed,
His rigor seemed quite permanent, and soon
She saw his prior engorgement had been because he was dead
Which shocked and dismayed poor
Mrs Ravoon!

350.
Unaware of necrophilia, the townsfolk partied on
They staggered gaily all around the toon
There was dancing, there was drinking, even sillier, hoots mon,
A fight broke out over a macaroon;
The last one left uneaten it was a lovely hue,
Deep purple that was spotted with maroon;
Completely in the dark, the air turned slowly blue,
As on the hillside wept
Mrs Ravoon!

351.
A low moaning sound, turning into a screech,
Echoed above the lagoon.
The Creature, still rigid, its soul out of reach
Was dragged by its feet by crampoon.
Standing it up in the back of the cave,
For safekeeping, or use; a mad croon,
Escaped from the lips, o'er the quivering hips
Of the lust driven
Mrs Ravoon!

352.

Was it wonder or lust, that drove her to try
One more go with the poor rigid goon?
He stood in the corner, erect but not spry,
Stone frigid as she hummed a tune,
At once unmelodious, deathless and dry,
Rigor mortis had proved quite a boon,
The dead Creature speechless, but a small cry
Of relief, came from
Mrs Ravoon!

353.

Though content with the Creature, she sought something fresh,
And she fancied a curry tycoon
Might just fit the bill with his nice spicy flesh,
So she wandered down to the saloon,
But he wasn't there so she tried the snackbar
Newly opened in downtown Dunoon,
Where, behind the counter, stood handsome Akbar;
Drool fell from
Mrs Ravoon!

354.

Nonplussed at the presence of one who had hurled
His present into the lagoon,
Akbar's natural politeness unfurled,
He was pleasant and slow to impugn
The haggard old buzzard, whose small beady eyes
Gazed at him like some poltroon,
Lost in the moment, yet bile seemed to rise
As he stood up to
Mrs Ravoon!

355.

"Akbar", she cried, "You're so virile,
So sleek by the light of the moon,
Your manliness makes me feel senile,
Come to my cave, before noon."
The poor man was in a dilemma,
He wanted to help, but not soon,
From under his feet came a tremor,
From the vibrating
Mrs Ravoon!

356.

She lured the kind restaurateur back to her lair,
Where he noticed that there, in the room,
Stood in the corner quite naked and bare,
Gathering dust, was her former bridegroom.
Every hair on his head stood up on its end
Like stiff bristles on a witch's broom,
He yearned to escape and did not wish to spend
One more moment with
Mrs Ravoon!

357.

Akbar stood horrorstruck, quite petrified
Yet like Gordon, who defended Khartoum,
He stood his ground, looked around, and then sighed:
"This cave is the home of a loon,
It is so dusty, so cobwebbed and dark,
I fear it resembles a tomb."
As he set to work with a duster, a spark
Of distaste came from
Mrs Ravoon!

358.

Dirt quickly diminished, but time passed by slow,
There was much to be done, yet by June,
Akbar hoped to be finished, for then he must go
As his wives would be missing him soon.
Meanwhile the resident, fire inside her,
Cackled like a crazed baboon,
As Akbar encountered an enormous spider
And in haste fled from
Mrs Ravoon!

359.

Down the hillside he ran, his duster in hand,
Over nettles, heather, and soon,
He heard the echo of footsteps that spanned
The expanse twixt the cave and Dunoon.
Though he was chaste, being chased by the hag
Made his virtue much like a balloon:
Easily popped, if for seconds he dropped
His distance from
Mrs Ravoon!

360.

He ran like the wind, his pace never slowing,
Pursued by that passionate loon
Who knew the terrain, and was intent on knowing
Both the thrill and the picayune,
Of his every contour, his brain and his bod,
Believing it written in rune,
That he should be hers; the choice, although odd,
Was as scripture to
Mrs Ravoon!

361.

While some succumbed to her weird charms, most ran for their
lives,
Though the rocky road ahead was roughly hewn;
Luckily for Akbar, his well-armed jealous wives,
Stood guard across the high street of Dunoon.
Standing there immoveable, clutching sharpened knives,
Vast in number, reckless, widely strewn,
Like angered bees defending the safety of their hives,
They hoped they could repel
Mrs Ravoon!

362.

She knew the backstreets, short-cuts, alleyways and such,
This inside knowledge proved to be a boon;
By devious distraction, death was dodged, and much
Confusion rained upon the wives' platoon.
She walked, unseen, behind them, then she strolled inside a
Warm and welcome snackbar new to toon,
Where sitting herself down, with a large and threatening spider,
The staff tried hard to please
Mrs Ravoon!

363.

She ordered ostentatiously, a veritable feast,
'Twas obvious this was no greasy-spoon;
The food was quite impeccable, with flavours of the east,
And she ate it like a ravenous racoon.
The staff were somewhat startled at the presence of the spider,
Which watched in silence, seemingly immune,
To the upset it was causing as it weaved a web far wider
Than the widest wife that sought
Mrs Ravoon!

364.

Forty irate women stood there, waiting in the street,
Outside the snackbar in downtown Dunoon,
Seething and impatient as they watched their victim eat
An endless stream of dishes with a spoon.
The more she ate the less it seemed her hunger did diminish,
Her stomach swelled like a barrage balloon,
Surely after one more course their nemesis must finish?
Nothing could hurry up
Mrs Ravoon!

365.

She smacked her lips and masticated one wafer thin mint,
Having eaten both lime jelly and stewed prune,
Though her stomach was distended, her features looked like flint,
As she rose and staggered slowly from the room.
The spider, which, beside her, followed gamely through the door,
Was the first to spot the wives, and a typhoon,
Of venom from its fangs was swiftly followed by a roar
From the poppadum-enhanced
Mrs Ravoon!

366.

All around was mayhem, Akbar's wives were quickly scattered,
As the street became a gigantic spittoon,
Each of them disgusted as they ran but were still splattered,
By a tidal wave of food, like a monsoon.
Half-digested morsels flew at them like putrid darts
Some even sought relief in the lagoon,
There was little question left that in warfare's deadly arts
Few were equal to
Mrs Ravoon!

367.

Akbar stood aghast, as his wives all reassembled,
He'd seen nothing of this kind before, yet soon
The realisation came to him that this whole scene resembled
A catastrophe in some horrid cartoon.
He tried his best to reason with the vomit-spurting hag
Whose manners seemed more fit for a baboon,
Meanwhile her wily spider threw a newly spun silk bag
O'er the women who opposed
Mrs Ravoon!

368.

Enmeshed in a sticky web, the women raised a cry
That was much more of a screech than 'twas a croon,
Their husband stood transfixed, too terrified to try
To battle with the nauseating loon,
Who had just been his customer, and treated with respect,
As befits one who frequents his proud saloon,
But this was an exception, he knew not to expect
Fair play from the befouled
Mrs Ravoon!

369.

Akbar laid a plan that was quite cunning:
To act just like an amiable buffoon,
And go up to the cave, instead of running;
Though terrified, he tried hard not to swoon.
Instead he offered to prepare a curry
So glorious his host would not impugn,
Nor detect, inspect, suspect, or even worry—
That he planned to tranquilize
Mrs Ravoon!

370.

A little dash of poppy seed, some opium and spice,
Were mixed in with the curry of cardoon,
Halfway through a plateful she declared it *rather nice,*
As she reached out for some pickles with a spoon.
Patient as a standing stone, Akbar simply waited,
As lazy clouds slid slowly passed the moon,
Until, replete with tranquilisers, bhajees, and quite sated,
A dreamless sleep fell on
Mrs Ravoon!

371.

Akbar did not hesitate; he ran off like the wind,
Down the mountainside to the lagoon.
The opium he'd used was the best; it had been tinned,
And sent by first class mail straight from Kowloon.
Its high content of alkaloids ensured that it was strong—
The finest of its kind, and what a boon!
Her fondness for the stuff meant he had done nothing too wrong;
He felt justified to flee
Mrs Ravoon!

372.

Untangling all his furious wives, from their spidery net,
Time not on his side, but good fortune
Brought a passing submarine—a Russian one, but yet
It might take them down the Clyde, and out of toon.
They hitched a ride, politely asking that the friendly crew
Point a periscope toward the wayward loon,
That lived up in the cave, who, watched and wakened, clearly knew,
But would revenge consume
Mrs Ravoon!?

373.

The submarine began to sink, and Akbar waved goodbye
To the town, and to his snackbar in Dunoon.
With barely enough time to think, he began to cry;
Such great beginnings ended with such gloom.
Though the Clyde looked quite magnificent, when seen from up
on high,
Its bed looked like the surface of the moon.
His forty wives could not care less, and exhaled a mutual sigh,
Hoping they'd forget
Mrs Ravoon!

374.

Seen from underneath the surface, all seemed quite serene,
The engines slowly turned, and fairly soon,
A notion of some forward motion in the submarine,
Was affirmed as they passed into the lagoon.
But standing on the hillside, with a fire in her belly,
And a hagfish in her hand, the raving loon,
In the cave, began to rave that all would turn to jelly,
As crazed laughter echoed from
Mrs Ravoon!

375.

Hurtling down the hillside in an opiated haze
With her hagfish in a watered, glass balloon,
She resembled some strange teenager caught in the latest craze,
And could easily have earned the odd doubloon,
Appearing on the cover of a Fortean magazine;
An example of a cave-dwelling old goon,
Instead, she was preoccupied, an unstoppable machine;
Nothing could impede
Mrs Ravoon!

376.

With an overarm technique, she hurled the bowl toward the water,
In hope it was a harbinger of doom;
A *message in a bottle* that anyone who fought her,
Would be pursued into their very tomb.
Against the sinking sub's grey hull, the glassy orb was shattered,
Sharp and splintered shards around were strewn;
All sense of proportion lost, revenge was all that mattered
To the solipsistic, mad,
Mrs Ravoon!

377,

Drinking gin on the quay, as the Clyde turned to gel,
Munching oats from a tin with her trusty old spoon;
The hagfish, now free, left a miasmic smell,
As she waited with glee for her nose to attune.
The stench overwhelmed all those inside the sub,
Its motors now stuck, it lay in the lagoon,
Helpless, as she wiped her hands on a shrub,
There were forty-one fearful of
Mrs Ravoon!

378.

Akbar rapidly pounded up spice,
As his wives tried to make a harpoon;
He intended to cook up the hagfish, with rice,
Some sauce, and samosas, as soon
As the Captain was able to open the hatch
From their jellified putrid cocoon.
Could it be that his cookery might make a batch
That would pacify
Mrs Ravoon!?

379.

A puncture wound brought forth a deluge of slime,
like black juice from a long-rotted prune,
At this juncture there seemed no reason or rhyme,
To the actions of this ectozoon.
Down in the galley the cooking began
Which created a splendid perfume,
Yet nobody really wanted to dally,
As they ran from
Mrs Ravoon!

380.

Akbar started slicing up the jelly
And stirred the pot with his large wooden spoon.
The resulting mixture proved to be quite smelly,
But with patience would be edible by noon.
He knew too well that one should never hurry,
Should take time to let the spices get in tune,
When one's life depends on boiling up a curry
With which to distract
Mrs Ravoon!

381.

The curry was done, the crew were all ready,
They opened the hatch—very soon,
The cool air was filled with a scent, warm and heady,
Which carried across the lagoon.
Out of sight, but quite close, with a plate in her hand,
Waiting silently by the pontoon,
Unaware of her plight, her feet on dry land,
overconfident:
Mrs Ravoon!

382,
The captain was Russian, and no diplomat,
Though he had no great wish to impugn,
All of the fussing, the *this* or the *that*
Which had delayed his flight from Dunoon.
The remaining gel thickened, the engines stuck fast,
While the old hag out by the pontoon.
Munched hagfish curry, he determined to blast
Out a passage from
Mrs Ravoon!

383.
As the mad old bat gnawed at her hagfish and rice,
With no thought of impending doom.
The captain installed a thermo-nuclear device
That would clear any blockages soon.
Nothing and no-one could stand in his way,
When the moment seemed most opportune
To detonate, and seal the fate, of the unaware
Mrs Ravoon!

384.
The captain stood proud with his finger on the button,
Looking forward to the almighty boom,
That would turn to cinders mankind, cow, and mutton,
Hagfish, cod, newt and racoon.
All of the trees that swayed in the breeze
Would be reduced to ashes, and soon,
There would be nothing left, none to feel bereft, of the atomised
Mrs Ravoon!

385.

No four-minute warning, no siren nor bell,
No shadow was cast by the moon,
A blinding white flash sent the whole place to hell,
As a cloud formed much like a mushroom.
The sub slipped away with crew, Akbar, and wives,
All intact, but as for Dunoon,
There was no telling yet how many lives
Had been lost due to
Mrs Ravoon!

386.

Split into molecules, each one in pain,
The void left behind seemed to loom.
Existence itself was a trick of the brain
Snuffed out at the whim of the goon,
Who captained the sub, not a man but a stub,
A mere note in the huge cosmic tune,
Did he really think he was rid of the stink?
In the ruins stood
Mrs Ravoon!

387.

Some radioactive atoms
Charged by ions that bounced off the moon,
Congealed into numerous stratums
Of one 'twas unsafe to assume,
Had been destroyed and eradicated
By the blast that had bleached the lagoon.
Mutated, they incorporated
A new form of
Mrs Ravoon!

Death Comes Calling: Edward J Sullivan

388.

Already a hybrid of human and spider,
And ageless, as if from rock hewn,
Now it seemed there was hagfish inside her,
Like some curious kind of quadroon.
Present danger by no means averted,
Or reduced to the merely jejune,
It paid not to have one's attention diverted
Too far from
Mrs Ravoon!

389.

Back in her cave as Akbar receded,
She reclined in an armchair framed with gadroon,
And couldn't help thinking she had succeeded,
As a nuclear winter fell over Dunoon.
He could keep his forty wives, dull and without feature,
While she, content in her catacomb,
Sidled up to the rigid Creature
Who, though dead, fulfilled
Mrs Ravoon!

390.

Exuding slime from every pore,
Exhausted 'neath the moon,
Luxuriant in sexual gore,
She slithered round the room,
The Creature stood there unresponding,
Stiffened in the gloom,
A curious and inhuman bonding
Filled
Mrs Ravoon!

391.

The present soon passed, the future became past,
She cast her mind to times in Cameroon,
When life had seemed more simple, her troubles just a pimple
On the backside of the darkside of the moon.
Insatiable, her needs were few and easy to fulfil—
A greasy bone, some drugs, a macaroon,
Were sufficient to stop her feeling queasy, faint, or ill;
Nostalgia seemed to mock
Mrs Ravoon!

392.

Radioactive particles drifted past the door.
The brightness of the light, gone; all was broon.
Her turn of mind had shifted, her heart cried out for more,
As she wandered aimlessly across the dune.
Her lover now a skeleton, in solitude she'd travel
In her dreams to distant places like Rangoon,
Where once she'd been content 'fore she started to unravel;
Rudderless, adrift,
Mrs Ravoon!

393.

Rubbing with a grubby finger, counting her remaining teeth,
Her gums felt like the surface of the moon:
Rugged on the surface, like a rancid soft cheese underneath,
Her breath smelt like a decomposed racoon.
Spindly hairless arms and legs were shivering with cold,
As she walked around the murky green lagoon,
Careless of the quivering sunken bodies ripe with mould,
Whose ghosts could not disturb
Mrs Ravoon!

394.
Her belly growling just like thunder, she was sick of slurping soup
Made from spiders, beetles, heather and cardoon.
So it was little wonder that she was cock-a-hoop
At the prospect of a dentist, coming soon,
To a venue close and handy, almost down the track
Leading from the cave into Dunoon,
She knew that with her teeth removed, there'd be no turning back,
But bleeding gums resolved
Mrs Ravoon!

395.
Drunk on gin she staggered in
To her dentist, one Dr Colquhoun,
Who disapprovingly smiled as if she were a child,
Reeling back as he surveyed the ruin,
Of blackened old stumps and crumbling lumps,
Which, altogether, were much like Puccoon:
An acrid emetic, fumes arose from the wench,
There was no stench like
Mrs Ravoon!

396.
The dentist had a hunch he was a victim
Of a cruel and unusual loon,
But he found her foul aroma addicting
And did free work that should cost a fortune.
He removed all her stubs and replaced them
With the fangs from a fresh dead baboon,
After all 'twould be sad just to waste them,
And they looked good in
Mrs Ravoon!

397.

Her new dental implants were itching
And, at moments which seemed opportune,
She distracted herself by twitching
In a dark corner of the saloon.
The extraction took place in the morning;
By the time it was late afternoon,
Putrefaction set in without warning,
Inflaming
Mrs Ravoon!

398.

Her jaw set tight against the night, rigid firm and muscular,
A hint of stubble glinting by the moon,
Chewing biltong in the half-light, demeanour now crepuscular,
Wet trails of spittle led from the lagoon.
Drooling from some codeine, an air of forced serenity
Betrayed an inner turmoil, until soon,
A stinking exhalation carried some whispered obscenity
As darkness fell upon
Mrs Ravoon!

399.

She bit down on the lifeless meat, to which she was allergic;
It was dry and dusty like some sandy dune.
The spittle brought on by this substance, close to thaumaturgic,
Came in quantities requiring a large spoon.
It had qualities about it that seemed almost magic,
Justifying the high price—one gold doubloon,
But heeding no advice, in a trice, results quite tragic,
Approached then overcame
Mrs Ravoon!

400.

No Christmas on the isthmus, the cave was dark and cold,
A stagnant smell, decay, hung in the room,
Her stocking hung, expectantly, as time itself grew old,
But Santa could not penetrate the gloom.
No turkey, pies, or crackers, only bowls of spider gruel;
A lonesome dinner 'neath the watery moon,
Lacking in nutrition serving only to refuel
The inner turmoil of
Mrs Ravoon!

401.

She held a bow of mistletoe above the Creature's head,
And, oh so gently, kissed it with a swoon.
Though the stench was quite repellent she refused that it was
dead,
And imagined that a spark would, somehow, soon,
Ignite extinguished life again, into the here and now,
To melt the inner core of her cocoon,
And from the brink of ecstasy bring fresh sweat to her brow;
A fevered hope still plagued
Mrs Ravoon!

403.

Stood on the cliff overlooking the abyss
A beckoning dark seemed to loom.
The dank and cold Creature had refused her a kiss;
All her drugs turned to goo in the spoon.
Poised on the edge past the dead privet hedge
She gazed at the deep black lagoon,
Her feet half way off the precipitous ledge
The ravine called for
Mrs Ravoon!

404.

Halfway down the cliff she espied a rare fossil,
And grabbed onto it, hoping that soon,
It would stem her descent, and like some apostle,
She'd return from the void; what a boon
It would be to the world, how superb and colossal,
Her wise contributions—the moon
Seemed with stars and with darkness merely to jostle,
For the attention of
Mrs Ravoon!

405.

Time sharpened barnacles cut into her hand
Causing her to lose grip of the dune.
She fell in flash and an almighty splash
Welcomed her to the icy lagoon.
In the dark briny deep, strange figures, asleep,
Waved at her, their skeletons strewn,
Discarded, bereft, lying where they'd been left;
Former victims of
Mrs Ravoon!

406.

On the cold ocean floor stood the bones of her sister,
Which plankton and kelp did festoon.
It wouldn't be true to imply she had missed her,
Reunion had come far too soon.
What once was concealed was no longer hid,
As her eyesight began to attune,
Then a tap on her shoulder, a tentacled squid,
Made a beeline for
Mrs Ravoon!

407.

The life of a cephalopod is rarely dull,
In their undersea briny commune,
But on the occasions when there is a lull,
Taking time out to act like a loon,
Passes the hours twixt eating and sleep;
Thus in the much vaunted lagoon,
Far out of sight, in the water so deep,
A squid taunted
Mrs Ravoon!

408.

Enthralled by its wonderful tentacled arms,
The sight of which caused her to swoon,
Mrs R! rapidly turned on her charms,
And grinned liked a dribbling old goon,
Tempting the squid into sub-marine play,
Submitting at once; very soon
Beneath the waves, and without delay,
It was wrapped around
Mrs Ravoon!

409.

Amazed at its stamina, tiring at last,
She reached for a rusty harpoon,
That lay on the seabed, as ghosts of her past
Gazed in silence beneath the pontoon.
Stabbing the squid, its tentacles frantic,
Suckers and gore were bestrewn,
As its dead body drifted out to the Atlantic
Downstream from
Mrs Ravoon!

410.

Covered in seaweed, the bones of the dead,
Did not judge as they swayed in the gloom.
No sense of remorse ever entered the head
Of the one who'd sent them to their doom.
Their bodies were blackened, dark as a Zulu,
With blank eyes that seemed to lampoon,
The ways of a woman who'd mate with Cthulhu:
The lust-driven
Mrs Ravoon!

411.

Tiring at last of the water,
And clambering onto the dune,
The one lesson her life had taught her
Was to never fold one's cards too soon.
If she'd been a woman for betting
She would wager that by the full moon
There'd be time for mayhem and bloodletting
At the cruel hand of
Mrs Ravoon!

412.

She could take no more as, washed up on the shore
A gurgling came from her womb.
It was sunny and bright, but despite the white light,
Her heart was as dark as the tomb.
Twitching inside, like an innocent bride,
Yet wrinkled much like an old prune,
There was no place to hide as a pain in her side
Spelled disaster for
Mrs Ravoon!

413.

Her attempt at extinction had ended in failure,
Hot blood, still inside her, maroon;
Not the softness of squid, but something much scalier
Appealed on that grey afternoon.
Summoning thoughts of survival at last,
To the Creature she climbed, up the dune;
It was clear she must do something drastic, and fast,
Cold resolve gripped
Mrs Ravoon!

414.

Turning her back on the dead left behind
In their watery graveyard commune,
It was those yet to come that haunted her mind,
And she had to be rid of them soon.
Grabbing a cutlass that lay on the floor
She felt like a growing cocoon,
So she sliced herself open, and spattered with gore,
Unrepentant bled
Mrs Ravoon!

415.

Writhing around upon the slick ground,
Her wound spouting like a monsoon,
It seemed there was little hope to be found;
The Creature looked on like a goon.
Spurting out egglets of unbidden squid
Which wriggled and twitched round the room,
All her blurred focus was set to get rid
Of the offspring of
Mrs Ravoon!

416.
Alone on the cold floor the future looked grave
A small meal would be quite a boon.
There were no provisions at home in the cave,
She lay there distraught, until soon
In desperation she opened her mouth
And scurrying forth from the gloom,
Some spiders walked in as the squid headed south,
Rescuing
Mrs Ravoon!

417.
Without hesitating she chewed on a spider,
Spitting legs out into the spittoon,
Meditating on what had ere been inside her,
She staggered around like a loon.
Through the wet mist she could see far below
A commotion down in the lagoon,
As hundreds of squidlings set forth; there'd be no
Seafood dinner for
Mrs Ravoon!

418.
With old spider webs she managed to stitch
The wide gaping wound she had hewn,
But gangrene set in, it started to itch,
And a terrible stench filled the room.
Fevered and frenzied, her brow dripping sweat,
She considered herself a buffoon;
Ruled by her passions, now spent, they might yet
Make a corpse out of
Mrs Ravoon!

419.

Befuddled by pain, bewildered with fever,
A wretched demise seemed to loom;
No opium handy that might relieve her,
Just spiders, the dead, and the gloom.
The smell of decay that arose from her gut
Told her that she must act very soon,
So with mosses and mud she plastered the cut;
The resourceful
Mrs Ravoon!

420.

Girding her loins and gritting her teeth
She took the path into Dunoon.
Her bandages catching on gorse from the heath,
Blighted trees silhouettes by the moon.
Down by the harbour she stepped on the ferry,
The crossing cost half a doubloon.
Thinking a day trip might be rather merry,
Sea air revived
Mrs Ravoon!

421.

Halfway across the fast-running Clyde,
The sound of a plangent bassoon,
Carried across the waters so wide
And the ferryman started to croon.
The sound was so moving a tear filled her eye;
To emotion she was not immune.
With a tremulous heart she exhaled a long sigh,
As remorse tempered
Mrs Ravoon!

422,

Turning to gaze from the opposite shore
At her home in the mountains she soon
Heard the splashing of water just once, then once more,
And looked down to the river so broon.
Dozens of tentacles waved with delight
At their mother who, like a cartoon,
Leapt in the air—the future seemed bright;
Optimism filled
Mrs Ravoon!

423.

Small rays of sunshine shone down on her head;
In the air was a pleasant perfume.
Considering that she had almost been dead,
She now bloomed in the fine afternoon.
Casting aside her rat-tailed wig
And grabbing a passing dragoon,
She ran through the fields while dancing a jig;
The revitalised
Mrs Ravoon!

424.

Thoughts of her childhood ran through her mind:
Sweets at the fairground in Troon;
The loss of her teeth, so long left behind,
From a fight in some distant saloon.
Filled with nostalgia tinged with regrets,
Some notable, some picayune,
She pitied her parents; only bad luck begets
A child like
Mrs Ravoon!

425.

Charity did not come easy to her;
She felt like a lonesome maroon.
Past good behaviour was lost in a blur,
And reflection just seemed to lampoon
A solitary life filled with venom and bile,
Where *strike first* was her signature tune.
Redemption, still distant, might take quite a while,
For the now pensive
Mrs Ravoon!

426.

Pondering how she could ever make good
Past mistakes, she raised up a platoon
Of poor homeless children with whom she would
Establish a peaceful commune.
An old run-down castle that stood by a stream
On a hillside that overlooked Scone
Provided the venue, it was a grand scheme,
Giving succour to
Mrs Ravoon!

427.

Suspicious of strangers, the children were scared
By the woman who hummed a weird tune.
Delicious gifts proffered seemed to show that she cared:
She passed biscuits round, cakes, macaroon!
Once tea time was over she put them to bed,
Where they slept till the next afternoon,
It was puzzling to ponder the thoughts in the head
Of the born-again
Mrs Ravoon!

428.

Days spent in laughter, in joy and in hope,
Lifted spirits; it was such a boon
To be free of the past, that familiar trope
Which had dashed all her chances so soon.
Gay happy children now danced all about,
Like sun-motes that swirled through the room,
What began as a whisper turned into a shout:
"Thank you so much, dear
Mrs Ravoon!"

429.

One little laddie was missing his mum;
His friends called him Hamish Colquhoun.
He cried out so woefully that she said, "Come,
I will take your hand, and very soon
You will see that the future looks cheerful and bright,
Once we're all settled in our commune."
The lad ceased his sobbing, and all was put right
By kindly old
Mrs Ravoon!

430.

By night she was plagued by peculiar dreams;
Vague obscurities written in rune.
Her past was now shaping her present, it seems;
Glistening shards, like glass smashed by a spoon,
Of memories, fantasies, worlds she had known,
Overtook her and shook her till soon
It was hard to distinguish the real from the grown;
As confusion vexed
Mrs Ravoon!

431.

Trying hard to be generous and pleasant,
In fields round-about she had strewn
Seeds of wildflowers meant as a present,
To emit a delightful perfume.
The innocent children sang as they picked
Small bunches to hang in their room,
But woe betide those who by bad luck had licked
Poppy heads grown by
Mrs Ravoon!

432.

Wee Hamish ingested the juice of the poppy,
He staggered, and then he fell doon.
His demeanour soon changed from contentment to stroppy;
Without it he wailed like a loon.
Try as she might she could not find a cure;
Neither hemlock nor mace or cardoon,
Seemed to restore his condition, once pure,
And dismay fell on
Mrs Ravoon!

433.

'Twas not on purpose; her intent was restricted
To help, love, and care, yet by June
All of the children she'd saved were addicted
To her poppy-sap flavoured majoun.
Still wishing to aid them, she hired a cab
To the airport to fly to Cancun,
Where all of the kids went into rehab,
All paid for by
Mrs Ravoon!

434.

The suffering children all went through cold turkey,
And shivered from night-time till noon;
Managing only mere scraps of beef jerky,
And small sips of soup from a spoon.
When days of delirium finally passed
There remained yet an oppressive gloom;
Despite all her kindness, cold glances were cast
At their poisoner—
Mrs Ravoon!

435.

Distraught at the damage and at her wits end,
She pled with the children, but soon,
As they turned their backs, she started to rend
Her hair as she howled at the moon:
"All of my efforts at kindness," she wailed,
"Have failed." She assailed a quadroon,
Whose churlish response, like a cruel dart, impaled
The bereft heart of
Mrs Ravoon!

436.

Knowing the children could not speak the tongue,
She corralled them and bargained them doon.
With persuasion and promises, all of the young
Were brought round by her visions, and soon
They were marching determinedly through the bright streets
As they made their way out of Cancun.
It was one of the greatest of all of the feats
Achieved by old
Mrs Ravoon!

437.

On their journey through town a man with a mask
Entertained them by playing a tune.
Keen to join in yet too frightened to ask,
As his face was a skull-like cartoon,
They asked the old lady if she had a peso
To spare for this busking buffoon.
"If I had a hundred I wouldn't say so,"
Growled miserly
Mrs Ravoon!

438.

For luncheon she munched on a raw jalapeno
And quickly desired a spittoon.
Her mouth was on fire; in pain she could see no
Relief, then a vinegaroon
Snuck up behind her, bit into her toe,
With a yelp she jumped up like a loon;
One could feel the appeal of old Mexico
Quickly fading, for
Mrs Ravoon!

439.

Unimpressed by the Mexican day of the dead,
To the charms of which she was immune,
There were corpses enough living on in her head,
Or waiting back home in Dunoon.
The music and laughter drove her to distraction,
As it wafted out from a saloon.
"This is no time for sightseeing, 'tis time for action,"
Insisted old
Mrs Ravoon!

440.

Gathering every spare bit of cash—
Ten pesos, a pound, a doubloon—
She hurriedly tried to replenish her stash,
A task which took all afternoon.
She sought out some scoundrels with something to sell,
But mistakenly tried to impugn,
The merchandise sold to her by the cartel,
Which was foolish of
Mrs Ravoon!

441.

Sanchez and Miguel were dangerous men,
Who had sold her some drugs and a spoon
In which to cook them; she did so and then
Asked for credit, promising soon
That she would return and have money to burn;
When the moment was most opportune,
But she turned and fled, and they both saw red;
They would not forget
Mrs Ravoon!

442.

Into the wilderness she led her tribe;
To the desert, where under a dune,
Due to incessant wheedling, plus the odd bribe,
They dug caves with the aid of a spoon.
The cold desert night made proximity snug;
The children invented a tune:
"Here in this cave we are free of the drug,"
Serenading tired
Mrs Ravoon!

443.

Days turned to weeks and food was quite rare;
They ate lizards, cacti, and racoon.
As night fell their guardian, brushing their hair,
Calmed them all with a gibbering croon.
It was clear her intentions were good, and yet still,
Doubts were surfacing; surely quite soon,
For want of nutrition someone would fall ill,
Jeopardising poor
Mrs Ravoon!

444.

Listening at length to a passing coyote
That hung by the edge of the dune,
(A vision conjured up by the peyote
They'd eaten that same afternoon),
Asking if it had any advice
To pass on to their creaking commune,
They heard of the hopelessness, and the high price
Paid for following
Mrs Ravoon!

445.

They scavenged all morning for half-eaten bones
Left by jackals who ate by the moon,
Until, without warning, their ravenous moans
Caused their leader's fraught mind to untune.
Pouring with sweat, she was heavily-scented;
The children were far from immune,
To the odour that came in waves from the demented
And highly strung
Mrs Ravoon!

446.

Ravaged by hunger the children ran wild,
They roved over desert and dune.
Instinct took over the mind of each child,
Bestial as a rabid baboon.
Some fell by the wayside, others were eaten
Skeletal remains mocked the moon.
Stood to one side, bowed but unbeaten:
Their governess,
Mrs Ravoon!

447.

Her small sullen family gathered around
Sharing scraps of dead meat, and cohune.
With blood on their chins but not making a sound
They agreed to return to Cancun,
Where appetite caused them to opt for mayhem;
There'd be hell to pay that afternoon.
As their leader proclaimed, "It is us, or it's them."
They all followed
Mrs Ravoon!

448.

Cleaving their way though the streets with blunt axes,
They encountered a raving pashtoon,
Who enquired of them whether they'd paid any taxes
Since making their home in Cancun.
The negative answer brought no good at all;
He reported them to the patroon,
It was obvious this could betoken the fall
Of the powerless
Mrs Ravoon!

Study for "The Pied Piper of Hamelin": The Children:
George John Pinwell

449.

Stuck like a pig, one child was a squealer,
And wailed as the ground turned maroon.
In desperation, and drunk on tequila,
As round her the children lay strewn,
She rallied her senses—the future looked bleak;
A pile of small limbs had been hewn.
Bloodstained and filthy, no-one wished to speak
To the traumatised
Mrs Ravoon!

450.

The adventures they'd had seemed to be a great jape
But 'twas clear they must end very soon.
Despairing, they looked for some means of escape,
So they hurriedly built a kytoon.
For those of you unsure of just what that is,
'Tis a cross twixt a kite and balloon—
With an almighty leap and a cry of *Gee Whizz*
They ascended, with
Mrs Ravoon!

450a.[23]

The beast from the east was the least of their worries
Although it was hardly a boon,
A feast she had planned never ceased—they had curries
Served by Akbar with his silver spoon
But a pest from the west proved a much harder test
It came in the shape of a glutton
Who in haste laid to waste all the food it could taste:
Poppadoms and lychees, curried mutton.
Up in the clouds, wrapped up in shrouds,

23 In response to Sylvia and Liz

'Gainst the icy blasts, cold as the moon,
They watched the snow falling below
While inside their tummies all was aglow
As they hurled out the pest onto an icefloe
And passed around puddings, to and then fro
Laughing at fate as the four winds did blow
Even Frosty the snowman just didn't know
He was never as cool as the weatherman's foe:
The full-up but frost-bitten
Mrs Ravoon!

451.
Gazing down from their refuge up in the air,
It took moments for them to attune
To this brand-new perspective, then, free of care
They sang out, "We've escaped from Cancun."
But danger soon found them, as from the south-west
Came a raging and violent typhoon,
Which gave no respite, and no hope of a rest,
For the wind-beaten
Mrs Ravoon!

452.
Thunderclaps, lightning, it stormed and then showered.
Wet through, and lit up by the moon,
Whimpering down in a corner there cowered
The trembling Hamish Colquhoun.
Sick of the sound of his weeping she'd sworn
She would jettison him—he'd be strewn
Over both land and sea; his wailing had worn
Down the patience of
Mrs Ravoon!

453.

"Please take me home," he attempted to scream
"Back to my friends in Dunoon."
Only for want of oatcakes and ice-cream
Had he taken the trip to Cancun.
He'd fallen foul of that fatal addiction
To poppy juice—how picayune
That he'd be the victim of unwanted friction
Brought on by
Mrs Ravoon!

454.

The children gazed on the scene all aghast
And shrank from the rampaging loon;
Looking as one at the place where they'd last
Seen their little pal Hamish Colquhoun,
Whose body'd descended like lead to the ground
As it dropped from the makeshift balloon,
Without so much as making a sound
That might disturb
Mrs Ravoon!

455.

As Hamish was falling he reached in his pocket,
Finding half an oatcake, one doubloon,
An old lollystick he had carved like a rocket,
And sundry debris. "What a boon,"
He thought to himself as he pondered his biscuit,
"It's still a long way to fall doon;
Should I eat it now? I think I shall risk it."
Receding from
Mrs Ravoon!

456.

A far distant thud on the rocks, then a splash,
Was heard far below the kytoon.
Hamish had bounced from the beach; with a smash
His head broken—pipped like a prune!
The ocean then took him; he finally rested
On the seabed, where he was immune
To any regrets of the time he'd invested
Following
Mrs Ravoon!

457.

Wee Hamish had died without once more tasting
An ice cream or oatcake, and soon
His memory faded; his small body wasting;
Munched by fish in the bay of Cancun.
'Twas far from the land he had cared to call home;
His absence still felt in Dunoon,
Where nary a trinket, a photo, or bone
Would be sent on by
Mrs Ravoon!

458.

Dismayed by their guardian's violent behaviour
The children conferred, until soon
One of them piped up "she is no saviour,"
And the old lady's face turned maroon.
A mutiny now could prove deadly, or worse;
They clutched to their flimsy balloon.
There was not one among them who was averse
To despatching
Mrs Ravoon!

459.

Reviled by the children her life became hell,
As she struggled to steer the balloon.
Behind them, unnoticed, came the cartel
Who, through fear, ruled the roost in Cancun.
Sanchez and Miguel, intent on pursuit,
Had followed the crew just as soon
As they'd seen the departure of the hirsute
Absconding
Mrs Ravoon!

460.

Hovering high o'er the deep blue Atlantic
The threat of downfall seemed to loom.
The Mexicans nearing, she became frantic;
Dodging her debt augured doom.
The only recourse that seemed sure to succeed
Was to rise through the clouds, t'ward the moon,
Through rarefied air her craft gathered speed
But they still closed on
Mrs Ravoon!

461.

The ballast was heavy, their buoyancy nil,
'Twas imperative she should act soon.
And so she swallowed the bitterest pill,
Coldly eyeing her nervous platoon.
At knifepoint she forced the children to leap;
One by one they fell from the balloon,
Coming to rest 'neath the waters so deep;
Yet, ascending, was
Mrs Ravoon!

462.
It was obvious things had not gone as she'd planned;
All alone now, she steered the kytoon.
Sanchez and Miguel, both heavily tanned,
Hearts like stone, leered at her. With a broom
She waved them away, only pausing to say,
"Go to hell, I am bound for the moon."
But their spirits were up, they intended to slay
The penurious
Mrs Ravoon!

463.
As she passed through a cloud she hummed out aloud
A foul and malevolent croon
Which assaulted the ears of the Mexicans proud,
Who could not quite pinpoint the tune.
'Twas not mariachi, fandango, or twist,
But the screech of a banshee, and soon
Their resolve was full-set that they could not exist
On the same plane as
Mrs Ravoon!

464.
The thin wicker cradle suspended below,
Tethered tight to the windswept balloon,
By a weak makeshift cable which offered no
Support to the fugitive goon,
Felt creaky and worn, insecure and unstable;
It slowed down her progress till soon
The two angry Mexicans found they were able
To catch up with
Mrs Ravoon!

465.

As it flew past her she'd grabbed a large bird
Which, now brandished, its feathers wide-strewn,
Held at bay her pursuers as she tried to gird
Her loins till a time opportune,
When she might be able, through use of its beak,
To pierce her assailants, who soon
Were asking themselves, "What kind of freak
Is this harridan
Mrs Ravoon!?"

466.

The vulture she grasped was enraged as it fluttered
Its wings in disgust. Pretty soon
Locked in a fight with the crazed bird she muttered,
"If only I had a spadroon."
The Mexicans, spotting their moment, advanced,
Lunging hopefully with a harpoon;
A weapon which they felt clearly enhanced
Their chances 'gainst
Mrs Ravoon!

466a.[24]

Dear Yvie, it was kind to offer your tooth
For sale, you might think I'm a loon
But I live in a cave—that's odd but the truth—
In a faraway place called Dunoon.
I write poems all about teeth every morning;
To buy yours would be quite a boon.
I hope you will sell me it. Now I am yawning,
Must go. love
Mrs Ravoon!

---

24 For Yvie who is brave with teeth

467.

Punctured and pierced, it's fabric in tatters,
From the sky fell the broken kytoon.
Her mind was now focussed on practical matters:
She knew it would crash very soon.
Underneath was a beach, just out of reach,
But with luck she might swim for a dune;
When it came to survival no-one could teach
Very much to
Mrs Ravoon!

468.

With a bump and a crash she quickly landed,
Coming to rest on a dune.
The improvised craft was now smashed, she was stranded
On a small island just off Cancun.
Shortly thereafter her enemies came
Seeking recompense; they were immune
To all claims of poverty, pled without shame
By the handwringing
Mrs Ravoon!

469.

There on the beach stood her enemies, cruel,
Their faces lit up by the moon.
Sanchez and Miguel demanded a duel
But her weaponry lay widely strewn.
Unarmed and unable to do them much harm
She gurgled and gazed like a goon,
Then, clearly unstable, she turned on the charm;
Second nature to
Mrs Ravoon!

470.

The Mexicans wondered how they could prevent,
Or make themselves somehow immune,
To the unfurling of this unwelcome event
And they wished they'd stayed in their saloon.
Standing before them quite naked and pink,
With a hide like the skin of a prune,
She offered herself through a miasmic stink;
They were transfixed by
Mrs Ravoon!

471.

With a glint in her eye and froth on her lips
She suggested they all should lie doon.
Suggestively wiggling her old bony hips,
And emitting a hideous croon,
Sanchez and Miguel took it in turns
To despoil her; oh what a boon
Was the post-coital rest on the sand 'neath the ferns
That quivered o'er
Mrs Ravoon!

472.

Moving with stealth as the Mexicans slept,
She inched her way down the dune,
Muttering under her breath, "Jesus wept,
I must do away with them soon."
Looking around as the vagabonds snored,
Finding razor clams by a pontoon;
With both hands now armed she cackled and roared,
"You should not have chased
Mrs Ravoon!"

473.

Sanchez and Miguel woke with a start;
Through the shadows a threat seemed to loom.
Slitting a throat, a stab to the heart
Brought forth gallons of blood, spelling doom.
The edge of the razor clam sliced and then hacked;
Her hands dripped with liquid, maroon.
Though she was now free a nagging doubt racked
The overworked
Mrs Ravoon!

474.

Freed from pursuit, the Mexicans beaten,
Her troubles returned all too soon
In the form of great hunger—she had not eaten;
A bowl of broth would be a boon.
Preparing the bodies would pose little trouble,
And boiled with clams and cardoon,
A feast could be had—soon a stew was a-bubble,
And a belch came from
Mrs Ravoon!

475.

Discarding the bones, which she threw in some marshes,
She chewed on the meat and cardoon,
But she drew the line at the bristling moustaches
Like hairy worms, there, on her spoon.
Spitting them out with a look of distaste
She took stock; she was now a maroon
Alone on the island, new trials would be faced
By the world weary
Mrs Ravoon!

476.

Standing alone on the edge of the isle,
Gazing out into the gloom,
There was nothing inside that might raise a smile,
Not a twitch came from her barren womb.
Under the sea lay the children she'd lost;
It was evening and night would come soon.
Not a thing that she'd gained had been worth the cost;
Bitter tears fell from
Mrs Ravoon!

477.

Woken at dawn by the surf from the sea,
Having spent the whole night on a dune,
She spied something floating; it seemed to be
The body of Hamish Colquhoun.
Looking round frantically she grabbed a rope
Which hung from the nearby pontoon,
And lassoed the corpse which gave rise to fresh hope
In the strange mind of
Mrs Ravoon!

478.

The cadaver, though mouldy, led to a thought
That might save the day, and so soon
She gathered her wits and decided she ought
To preserve the small body. By noon
'Twas her considered view it would make a nice feature
If stood in the cave in Dunoon,
Where in pride of place, right next to the Creature.
It could watch over
Mrs Ravoon!

Wicked Woman: Francisco Goya

479.

Well versed in that finest of arts, taxidermy,
She gathered her tools, and yet soon,
Having tried using mud (the ground was too wormy)
She now improvised—with a spoon.
Lost in a haze of aesthetic depravity,
And toiling that whole afternoon,
She stuffed tiny twigs in his internal cavity;
"That's the ticket," cried
Mrs Ravoon!

480.

Wee Hamish now made a wonderful mummy,
His guts on the beach, widely strewn,
Pecked by birds. He stood, twigs in his tummy,
Which from tropical trees had been hewn.
Hefting him proudly on her scrawny shoulder,
She carried him to the pontoon,
Where they sat together beside a large boulder;
Dead Hamish, and
Mrs Ravoon!

481.

On the horizon she spied something odd,
Shapes of grey seemed to squeak from the gloom.
Great numbers of dolphins, massed in a pod,
Were approaching until, very soon,
She noticed each animal carried a child
It had rescued, once they had been strewn
'Cross the ocean. Now harried emotions ran wild
As they recognised
Mrs Ravoon!

482.

It seemed like a dream; the children were living
Despite their fall from the balloon.
But in the grand scheme, would they be forgiving,
Or seek their revenge on the loon,
Who had taken them all on a trip 'cross the globe
From the orphanage back home in Troon?
Soaking wet from the water, she helped them disrobe,
But not one trusted
Mrs Ravoon!

483.

In the morning the dolphins played tricks in the bay,
And beckoned them; "Won't you come doon?"
Speaking with clicks they seemed to say
"We can ferry you back to Dunoon."
'Twas an offer that no-one required to hear twice,
What a miracle, oh what a boon!
At last they had won one throw of Fate's dice,
"Homeward bound," shouted
Mrs Ravoon!

484.

Clambering onto the dolphins so sleek,
Their noses as grey as the moon,
The thought that they might have to sit there all week
Caused the strongest of children to swoon.
There'd be many perils on the journey back home
To the welcoming mists of Dunoon;
They swore that once there they no more would roam,
Or wander with
Mrs Ravoon!

485.

They sped like the wind across dangerous waters,
Baked by sun then lit up by the moon,
Salty spray soaking the sons and the daughters
Missing so long from Dunoon.
Dining on eels in the sargasso sea,
Which they sliced up and ate with a spoon,
Misadventures aside, they were all glad to be
Heading home; even
Mrs Ravoon!

486.

The dolphins made haste as the children clung tight;
To pass time they all joined in a tune,
But it soon became clear there was something not right
With their little pal Hamish Colquhoun.
Were he silent because of his irksome ordeal,
They could cheer him, but no—like the tomb
He gave no response to their calls—was he real?
Or a construct of
Mrs Ravoon!?

487.

Clutching wee Hamish she sped through the night,
Reassuring the children that soon,
All of their hardships would now be put right;
She grinned at them like a baboon.
Her razor sharp teeth and her sallow demeanour
Flashed like flint by the light of the moon.
The children could hardly believe they'd once been a
Near-family to
Mrs Ravoon!

488.
The dolphins behaviour became very strange;
As they swam in large circles and soon,
They appeared to be lost, their clicks underwent change,
Crazed barking ensued; a racoon
Appeared out of nowhere, the sky had two suns,
And what had become of the moon?
Much to their chagrin it seemed everyone's
Hopes lay with
Mrs Ravoon!

489.
A wild sea raged but the children held fast,
Placing their faith in Neptune.
The violent storm subsided at last;
Golden light penetrated the gloom.
An eerie calm made the sea like a table,
Fresh made yet abandoned. By noon
Some were unwilling, others unable
To move
Even Mrs Ravoon!

490.
Rain drizzled upwards, the compass was crazed,
Although she had slept until noon,
The old lady, in a daydream, now lazed
As she whistled *Au clair de la lune*
The children, bewildered, looked round in despair,
It was snowing, despite being June,
The dolphins still circled, and barked without care.
"Not a prayer," mumbled
Mrs Ravoon!

491.

The children, once docile, now became ruder,
Their whole world seemed like a cartoon.
To the south lay the tropical isle of Bermuda,
They howled their laments at the moon.
With the edges of sanity each seemed to wrangle,
Some silently, some with a croon,
The only constant in this devil's triangle:
The cackling of
Mrs Ravoon!

492.

She brave-faced the elements, wholly at ease;
In the midst of confusion, immune
To turbulent turmoil which seemed to tease
Fresh disaster from black roiling spume.
The dolphins, in panic, circled and snapped,
Seemingly set to consume
À la ouroboros, forever entrapped
In a cycle with
Mrs Ravoon!

493.

Revolving at great speed like a spindle on a spool,
Causing currents to head southwards, ever doon,
The resulting clash of energies formed a great whirlpool
Which by chance allowed their journey to resume.
Sucked into a vortex by immeasurable power,
Nature's brute vitality a boon,
That spat out yet more fiercely with every passing hour,
Dolphins, children, and
Mrs Ravoon![25]

---

25 *Editor's note: at this point, abruptly, the pome cycle came to its end, with the exception of the two side pomes printed on the next page. As Tim wrote when he uploaded the collected pomes in May 2018:*

> Yes, 493 complete pomes bringing her adventures bang up to date. I suspect this may be auspicious in the sense of suggesting new adventures on the horizon, but for the moment she remains in a puzzling void... Dare you read them again? Will she make good her promises? Can she ever return to Dunoon? All of these questions and more remain unanswered! How can you resist?

Side Pomes: 493a & 493b

From out of the blue came an insect
Both enormous and black as a prune.
The kind of thing she'd had to dissect
When at school as a child in Dunoon.
To the innocent eye it was horrid,
But depravity changed this till soon
Erotic notions so torrid
Overtook Mrs Ravoon

She fed it on rock cakes, bewitching
Its senses, until like a loon
The insect was horribly twitching
And dribbling like some old poltroon.
Acidic juices were flowing,
Ghastly spittle around was bestrewn,
A horrible stench started growing
Emitted by Mrs Ravooon!

*This book was put together from the original MSS
by the following friends of Tim Rundall:*

Liz Elliot, Mike Hardaker, Jeremy Smith, Rick Beets and Andrew Thomas

Printed in Great Britain
by Amazon

11488784R00113